What the Critics Say about Robert Anton Wilson

"Marshall McLuhan closed the book on printing press literature and predicted what Robert Anton Wilson has now produced -- a multi media para-graphic motion picture script. *Reality* is an historic event -- comic and profound. The next step is to put this masterful essay onto all our big screens."
— Dr. Timothy Leary, psychologist

"Robert Anton Wilson comes to the present from the future, seeing the incredible foibles of our species with the humor, compassion, and insights of an extraterrestial anthropologist. *Reality* is, unbelievably . . . true."
— Barbara Marx Hubbard, World Future Society

"With his humorous rapier, Wilson pokes and prods our misconceptions, prejudices, and ignorance. A quantum banquet."
— Ray Tuckman, Broadcaster, KPFK-Radio

"A profound book that reveals with raw humor the intrinsic inconsistencies in the thought systems underlying much of the craziness in our society."
— Peter Russell, author of *The Global Brain* and *The White Hole in Time*

"I'm a Christian; I hope Wilson is wrong. Funny, though."
— Marshall Fritz, Principal, Pioneer Christian Academy, Fresno, California

"A super-genius . . . he has written everything I was afraid to write."
— Dr. John Lilly, psychologist

"One of the funniest, most incisive social critics around, and with a positive bent, thank Goddess."
— Riane Eisler, author of *The Chalice and the Blade*

"A very funny man . . . readers with open minds will like his books."
— Robin Robertson, *Psychological Perspectives*

"A 21st-century Renaissance Man . . . funny, wise, and optimistic . . . the Lenny Bruce of philosophers."
— *The Denver Post*

"One of the most important writers working in English today . . . courageous, compassionate, optimistic, and original."
— Elwyn Chamberling, author of *Gates of Fire*

"Wilson does for quantum mechanics what Durrell's Alexandria Quartet did for relativity, but Wilson is funnier."
— John Gribbin, physicist

REALITY IS WHAT YOU CAN GET AWAY WITH

A Screenplay
by Robert Anton Wilson

A DELL TRADE PAPERBACK

A DELL TRADE PAPERBACK

Published by
Dell Publishing
a division of
Bantam Doubleday Dell Publishing Group, Inc.
666 Fifth Avenue
New York, New York 10103

The trademark Dell® is registered in the U.S. Patent and Trademark Office.

ISBN: 0-440-50332-9

Printed in the United States of America

Published simultaneously in Canada
May 1992

10 9 8 7 6 5 4 3 2 1

Acknowledgments

Many thanks to the following for their help in locating the photographs used in this book: The Academy of Motion Pictures Arts and Sciences, American Stock Photography, Collectors Book Store, Ohlinger's Bookstore, Photofest, Larry Edmunds Cinema & Theatre Bookshop, The Mary Pickford Collection, The Bettmann Archive, and UPI/The Bettmann Archive.

Almost all the stills used in this book were originally issued to publicize or promote films or TV material made or distributed by the following companies, to whom we gratefully offer acknowledgment: Universal Studios, Four Crown Productions, Turner Entertainment, Twentieth Century Fox, Columbia Television, Allied Artists, London Films, MosFilm, Columbia Pictures, DCA, Monogram Pictures, Paramount Pictures, Turner Entertainments/Warner Bros., G&N Productions, and Lucasfilm Ltd.

Special thanks to Sandy Ferguson of Legwork for photo research, Michael Flint for line art, Sebastian Orfali and Ginger Ashworth of Ronin Publishing for typesetting and packaging, Anand Singh Khalsa for providing photographs of the author, and Generic Typography for providing the scanning and montage work of the photographs and final imagesetting to film.

Introduction

by Professor Padraic Hakim Hasagawa,
University of New Dublin, Sirius 23

The screenplay presented here represents one of the strangest products of the late pre-Migration period of human history. Scholars agree that it dates from the 59th Century A.M. (called the 20th Century by the pagans of that period), but all else about it remains wrapped in obscurity, controversy, and enigma since it seems nearly impossible for civilized persons today to understand the superstitions and savagery of our earliest progenitors.

The 59th Century came near the end of the pre-dawn age of purely terrestrial ("closed system") history and has the designation "the Age of Bullshit" among paleo-anthropologists, for reasons that most first-year archaeology students seem singularly unable to grasp. However, with effort and imagination, recalling what we all learned in Comparative Primate Studies, we can recreate what the Bullshit Era meant to those who lived then, and especially to those who achieved the coveted rank of Bullshit Artist.

"Bullshit," the primary mode of communication in that age, has defeated the average student's attempt at analysis because it does not seem to function as a language at all. First, then, we must recognize Bullshit as a unique language or argot that predates all *modern* concepts of speech and information. We must think in archaic categories and forget that *information transfer* seems to us the natural function of communication. To primitives, it seems otherwise. Not information, but *disinformation*, preoccupied their lives. Thus, Professor Jubela has won universal academic consent to his proposal that Bullshit speech consisted in "saying that which is not so"—a "wild" and (to most naïve students) unthinkable concept.

Nonetheless, it appears that most humans of that period spoke almost entirely in Bullshit, and that whatever the laws or grammar of that language, it did not have, or attempt to have, any isomorphism or meaningful connection with nonverbal actuality. For our purposes, lacking the ability to comprehend fully the Dark Ages, an intuitive understanding of Bullshit can rely on Professor Jubela's oxymoronic approximation—"saying that which is not so."

To take a simple example: "I have my hand in your pocket and intend to steal your wallet" seems like a normal (if reprehensible) sentence to us; but in

Bullshit, this would seem unspeakable and (to some extent) unthinkable. A Bullshit translation would read something like, "I have come to protect you, and you owe me $5,000 for this service." Two major groups of Bullshit Artists, known as the Morphia (or Marphia?) and the CURS (or URS) employed this technique extensively. Realize that the function of Bullshit lies in concealing the facts, especially uncomfortable facts, and you begin to enter the reality-tunnel of this astounding ancient semantics.

Similarly, in Unistat, a special group of people, engaged chiefly in shooting, bombing, burning, and otherwise destroying other people, did not call themselves the Department of Murder or even the Department of War. These terms make no sense in Bullshit. Those engaged in that bloody profession called themselves the Department of Defense. Again, the function lies in concealing, not revealing, the facts.

Deep meditation on this second example will help the student enter imaginatively into the mental world of our anthropoid ancestors, back in the 59th Century when the Bullshit Artists ruled the world.

Now, as to the screenplay itself—

Professor Sven Giorgio Chung recently unearthed "stills" from this strange film—in the same archaeological dig, called Bev-El or perhaps Beve'hill, in the southernmost part of West Unistat, where the script itself came to light, together with most of the evidence we have of the movie industry of that barbaric age. Alas, these photos—which we include here as archaeological curiosities—only deepen the mystery and the endless debate about this film, because some of these photos contain historical figures known to have achieved the rank of Bullshit Artist (Eisenhower, Hitler, Reagan, Quayle), and nobody has explained why these personages found it necessary to earn spare cash appearing in what bears all the earmarks of a low-budget motion picture. Perhaps the widespread "thievery" of the Bullshit Artists (*politicians*, in the patois of that time) resulted from the low salaries these functionaries received, although I must admit that that conjecture represents pure speculation.*

————————————

* *Some claim these persons were edited into the film by "camera trickery," but this theory fails of conviction, since nobody has been able to explain how such "trickery" was accomplished.*

What we do know, or think we know, about the 59th Century After Mung indicates that films, like other artworks, fell under the supervision of a legendary Bullshit Artist named Jesse Helmer or Jesus Helmes or something like that. This man evidently believed that the Bullshit Artists, having attained eminence above all other (and hence, lesser) Artists, had the "Divine Right" to police the Arts in general. It appears that no film could be released (and no book published or painting exhibited) without the approval of this Bullshit Artist—probably also known as Archon or Emperor, or some similar title.

In addition, most (but not all) of that era's films received financing through Japanese and Swiss banks, but production fell to a group of "experts" in the aforementioned Southwest of Unistat (or, as Professor Jubelo would have it, United Stat). Contemporary glyphs portray these "experts" (producers, directors, and the like) as deranged abusers of the primitive neurochemicals of that age and as insatiable erotomaniacs; how they ever finished any of their films remains the greatest unsolved mystery about them.

Even in those Dark Ages, however, this film received no backing from the orthodox movie industry, and scholars (except the eccentric Professor Jubelum) agree that financing came from one of the many lunatic religious "cults" of the age, called the Erisian Liberation Front, or ELF. The production company, Miracle Films, is known only for this singular work and for a strange, abstract, almost plotless film called *Insatiable,* in which an actress named Marilyn Chambers performs various acrobatic or aerobic feats for approximately an hour. Nobody has yet been able to explain *Insatiable,* and we can only assume that certain kinds of acrobatic and/or yogic performances had an artistic or religious meaning for those primitives. None of the contortions of this Marilyn Chambers have any interest today, since they consist only of quite ordinary mating rituals.

We know no more of Miracle Films, except for its typically Aristotelian slogan, "If it's a good film, it's a Miracle."

---

* *No form of organized partnership society existed in those days, so bands of predators "ruled" over the masses. See "farmers" and "cattle" in any archaeological dictionary for descriptions of rulers and herds respectively.*
** *No true knowledge of the universe having appeared among them yet, these unfortunate folk relied on those with the best "line" of pseudo-explanations. Groups that shared the same delusions called themselves "churches."*

Evidently, the Erisian Liberation Front, the financiers of the present script, worshiped Eris, the Goddess of Chaos—a fit divinity for that hellish age, when disorder still appeared as the primary feature of existence and humans had not yet discovered any real Scientific Laws. All records indicate that "governments"* and "churches,"** along with truly powerful groups like the multinational corporations, followed the guidance of pseudo-scientists such as astrologers, geneticists, psychologists, Computer Wizards, readers of chicken entrails, and of course, the legendary Bullshit Artists. The masses followed such cults as ELF, the Sub-Genius Foundation, Crosstianity (which worshiped an implement of capital punishment), the Javafarians, and others.

Gilhooley's General Field Theory, the foundation of science as we know it, did not appear until at least a generation, or perhaps two generations, after this film.

We have here, then, a record of humanity on the edge of civilization but still sunk in ignorance, savagery, and squalor. The historical importance of this record hardly needs stressing. As we read, we can see, vividly, in our imaginations, the Missing Link between the apes and ourselves. We see the ordinary man and woman of the time, and we see the Bullshit Artists who ruled them.

Two technical terms need definition, of course. *Cut*, we now know with certainty, meant that the film would stop and the audience could have a sex break or go to the lavatory. A *tracking shot* indicated a sequence of film with railroad tracks crossing the screen, in the manner of the Abstract Paintings of that time.

It still remains to say a few words about the general history of that barbaric epoch, which may help guide the reader. Several "governments" (organized bands of Bullshit Artists) already had some crude rockets, but Migration had not yet begun: humanity remained confined to one harsh and backward planet. Finding the conditions there dreadful, humans assumed that *the universe* contained a basic flaw, and most of their intelligence, such as they had, went to the single task of explaining why the universe did not function properly. The Doctrine of the Original Snub, as given in this screenplay, seems typical of these pseudo-explanations. (A similar, but cruder, doctrine appears to have had the name Original Sin, but nobody today understands that. The only definition of *sin* that we have found, in a fragment of a book by somebody named Thorne Smith, describes it as "forgetting to pull down the shades."*)

---

* *Taboos based on closing windows or doors, secluding menstruating females, spilling salt, etc., exist among the Higher Barbarians on many planets.*

Of course, the problems of these primitives resulted from the finite resources of a single planet, or as we call it, "closed system technology." Since they had not yet achieved Migration, they could not even imagine the infinite resources available in the interstellar "open system technology." Thus, they divided into two major groups—those who spent their time "explaining" why humanity seemed doomed to failure, and those who, not bothering about explanations, set out to capture the limited resources available on one planet, so that they could be rich and comfortable personally, even if the rest of humanity starved.

The latter group, evidently, proceeded by brute force throughout most of history, but toward the end of the Dark Ages, they invented disinformation as a tool of plunder. In other words, by "saying that which is not so," they could steal without the use of force, in some cases, or with only the veiled threat of force, barely mentioned, lurking behind the disinformation. Some scholars posit that the linguistic machinations of this predator group necessitated the invention of the language of Bullshit and the eventual emergence of the Bullshit Artist, an expert at preventing the majority from realizing how the trickier forms of robbery and fraud operated.

This system had gone on so long that most humans could not imagine any other; and no better system did appear until Larson's Star Drive opened the universe to Migration and "open system technology" became possible. Gradually, in an age of abundance and superabundance, "saying that which is not so" became unnecessary, and modern languages, based on the communication of information, gradually evolved.

Returning to the 59th Century: The two most popular Bullshit Artists of the period appear to have had the names Adenoid (or Adolph?) Hitler and Ronald Reagan (or Ray-Gun?). Many surviving glyphs praise them in the same extravagant language found in inscriptions, from three thousand years earlier, hailing various Sun Kings of the Neolithic Orient, and they seem to have achieved general recognition as the Supreme Bullshit Artists of the Aeon. A minority of dissenters seem not to have liked Hitler or Reagan at all, and scholarly opinion holds that this screenplay emanated from that dissenting minority. Other Bullshit Artists of the period, such as L. Ron Hubbard and J. Danforth Quayle, appear to have elicited even less respect from our unknown Bard, perhaps himself an official of the Erisian Liberation Front.

Mired in Superstition, speaking (and therefore probably also thinking) in Old High Bullshit, trapped on one scarcity-ridden and inhospitable planet, our ancestors of the 59th Century led lives that we can only summarize as nasty and dreadfully short. Our unknown Bard seems to have understood that the first step toward a solution of their problems lay in *getting off the planet,* but he also seems to have understood, wearily and wryly, that few of his superstitious contemporaries would understand this message. He therefore devoted more of his energy to trying to persuade, seduce, or cajole them into *thinking.*

This almost certainly explains why this film never went into general release—or, according to Professor Jubelo, why it opened in several cities and immediately got seized and burned by the Mind Police.

People today find it hard to understand the Mind Police, and historical records do little to clarify the matter. The leader of this group, as we said, appears to have held the name (or religious title) Helmer or Helmes (or Hitler?), but the group itself seems to have changed its designation several times and we see it called "the Holy Office of the Inquisition," "the National Endowment for the Arts," "the Hays Office" (?), or "the Partnership for a Brain-Free America," or we see it referred to merely by opaque initials such as "CIA," "FCC," or "DEA." Some even hold that the leader did not have the name Helmer or Hitler but something like Zar Q. Mada or Zar Bil Bennett.

Beyond all these historical puzzles, one fact does emerge: The Mind Police served the function of preventing humans from learning how to use the brain for fun and profit. The dogma of the time insisted that the brain should serve only to achieve misery and despair (a state known as "maturity"); this doctrine seems to have derived from the equally mysterious mythos concerned with the aforementioned Original Sin and/or the so-called Primal Scene (a related legend even less comprehensible than Original Sin). In simple language, the whole Mind Police apparatus, whether called FCC or DEA or whatever, seems to have served to maintain the norms of the Age of Bullshit and to abort any effort at clear thinking or plain speaking.

Many savants have pondered the identity and/or the "reality" of the personages in this screenplay. Professor Marie Jeanne Alhazred, an early authority, persuaded many scholars that the characters all derive from actual historical personages. In revolt against this theory, Professor Toshiro Luigi Murphy popularized the notion that the script consists entirely of the legends and myths of those Dark Ages. Both interpretations appear incomplete and one-sided in light of more recent scholarship, and we now believe that the mysterious author of these pages, like his near-contemporaries, Omer and Mock Twain, merrily mixed fact and fancy according to his own taste.

In the Age of Bullshit, the author's willingness to allow any fact into his script at all probably accounted for the rapid repression of the film.

A few words about key figures and their real or mythic origins seem in order.

Humphrey Bogart, one of the principal characters in this script, appears to have functioned as Hierophant or Pope or something of that sort, as indicated by many glyphs mentioning "the Bogart cult." We have reason to believe this religious leader, or Guru, appeared in several other films, all of them unfortunately lost. While we find it hard to comprehend how a person can serve a religious function and simultaneously work as an actor, this appeared not uncommon in the 59th Century After Mung. Ronald Ray-Gun and other persons known as Sonny N. Chair and Clint Westwood (or Eastwood) also appear to have held religious offices while working part time as entertainers.

Orson (or H. G.?) Welles appears to have worked as Hierophant or Sorcerer, but at some point he injudiciously showed his dupes how the tricks of magick work; this led to disillusionment and some bitterness, and it evidently cut short his career, although some evidence indicates that he went on to write many popular books about invisible men, wars between worlds, and genetic engineering. Some credit him also with an outline of prehistory.

Jane Russell, the most mysterious figure in the film, appears to have worked in the primitive brain research of that age, as the many references in the script make clear. Evidently, at one point, the two hemispheres of the brain had her name affixed to them.

Ignatz Ratskiwatski appears in only one other motion picture, called either *Of Morgan Creek* or *Of Human Bondage*. Strangely, although his name appears often in the dialogue to that film, he himself never appears on screen.

George Herbert Walker Bush appears to have held some high rank in a group
called Skull and Bones, but we do not know if this functioned as a "government"
or a "church." Evidently, as indicated in many surviving glyphs, he did not speak
the same Old High Bullshit as his contemporaries, but pioneered the language or
dialect later known as Middle Low Horseshit. This differs from OHB, in which
words "say that which is not so"; in MLH, words do not say anything at all. Some
hold that this purely aural or contentless speech led to the invention of music, but
other evidence suggests that music existed even before Bush and that he merely
pioneered the usage of purely musical structure in oratory, divorcing it not only
from "that which is" but also from "that which is not."

Popeye appears to have served as Pope or President in one of the major
"governments" or "churches." Historians remember him as "the one who liked
spinach," an easy mnemonic, distinguishing him from Bush, "the one who did
not like broccoli."

Betty Boop and/or Betty Boop Ratskiwatski appears to have emerged from
an early Fertility Goddess. Professor Madonna Veronica Kurasawa claims, with
some plausibility, that certain females served as "incarnations" of this Goddess
for a period of months or years and were then sacrificed. (See her "The Maiden
and the Dragon: The Legend of Marilyn Monroe," *Archives of Terran Archaeology*, XXXIII, 17.)

Shelley McClown appears a totally fictitious character, since we find no
other record of her. This delightful creation remains a favorite among students of
ancient language, since she speaks the most authentic dialect of Old High Bullshit
in the entire script.

In closing, it might help us to "place" this remarkable work if we note that,
about one hundred years before its composition, no rockets or even airplanes
existed, the average lifespan remained about fifty years, most people could nei-
ther read nor write, and poverty existed everywhere.

At the time of this work, rockets had reached a few planets, average lifespan hovered around seventy-six years, literacy had arrived in most of the planet, and the homeless poor survived only in Unistat and other "Third World" countries.[*]

One hundred years later, 1,200 space cities existed in the solar system, the first extrasolar colony neared completion in the Centauri system, lifespan had reached 240 years, and even on Terra no human had an income of less than a billion credits per lunation.

So here, then, you may read the fears, the hopes, and the strange, twisted humor of one unknown Bard who seems to have dimly intuited that he lived at the end of Earthly history and could see, even more dimly, the Cosmic History that lay directly ahead.

---

[*] *The term* Third World countries *refers to those with low industrial plant and high birth rate, where poverty and misery naturally prevailed. Professor Jubelum denies that Unistat belongs among the Third World countries, citing a few archaeological digs indicating some advanced technology there and a fragment of text calling Unistat a "rich" country. Nonetheless, the bulk of the evidence indicates that Unistat had vast poverty, armies of homeless wretches, no National Health plan, and all the other typical Third World characteristics. Professor Jubelum attempts to explain this by asserting the Unistaters spent their wealth entirely on weapons, but one finds it hard to credit the possibility of such a nationwide mental aberration even in that barbaric age.*

Reality Is What You Can Get Away With

A Screenplay

Aerial zoom shot of the Los Angeles freeway system under heavy smog.

Soundtrack: Ominous music suggests the ticking of a clock.

CUT TO: *Closeups of bumper stickers on cars:*

IF GUNS ARE OUTLAWED, ONLY OUTLAWS WILL HAVE GUNS
IF NUKES ARE OUTLAWED, ONLY OUTLAWS WILL HAVE NUKES
IF LAWS ARE OUTLAWED, ONLY OUTLAWS WILL HAVE LAWS
IF MARRIAGE IS OUTLAWED, ONLY OUTLAWS WILL HAVE INLAWS

CUT TO: *Montage of atomic explosions from newsreel films of nuclear tests. Repeat some shots in slow motion.*

Onscreen comes the (false) title, DEATH OF EARTH.

CUT TO: *Closeup of IGNATZ RATSKIWATSKI, his face contorted with death-agony.*

Camera pans back to reveal that IGNATZ is in bed, waking from a nightmare. He is an ordinary guy, around thirty-five, and does not look at all like a leading man or professional actor.

Camera pans in again to register IGNATZ showing dawning relief.

IGNATZ: Oh, Jesus, it was only a nightmare.

Camera pans back to reveal bedroom. White light flashes through the window, and a windstorm shakes entire room.

CUT TO: *Slow-motion shot of atomic explosion.*

CUT TO: *IGNATZ in pajamas running down empty pre-dawn street. Heavy sounds of panting. All around him, buildings are on fire. IGNATZ registers total terror.*

CUT TO: *JANE RUSSELL in haystack.*

CUT TO: *Closeup of* IGNATZ *in terror. Camera pans back to reveal he is still in bed, sitting up, coming out of "nightmare" to "reality."*

IGNATZ: Jesus motherfucking Christ, the same nightmare twice in a row. I only dreamed I was awake. (*Sudden suspicion crosses his face.*) Could it be happening again? Am I still dreaming that I'm awake?

Camera pans back to reveal full bedroom and zooms in on TV in corner. TV turns itself on, and we see the opening sequence again, from atomic blasts to the title, DEATH OF EARTH.

Camera pans back to IGNATZ.

IGNATZ: Am I dreaming I'm dreaming, or am I dreaming I'm awake?

Camera pans back to TV. We move in to closeup and the TV screen becomes a film screen. A professional handsome bland baritone ANNOUNCER *appears with yellow wall behind him. On wall is photo of Playmate of the Month.*

ANNOUNCER: We don't like to think of Death Of Ego . . . We disguise it in dozens of ways . . . even as Death Of Earth . . .

CUT TO: IGNATZ *in pajamas walking down a long, shadowy hall. A
                 door on the right side of the wall opens with a BOOM, and out
                 flies a flag with the giant initials* DOE.

IGNATZ: Death Of Ego . . . Death Of Earth . . .

*The flag flies back behind the door, which slams loudly (another BOOM), and we
see the end of the hall, an animated movie screen.*

CUT TO: *The animated screen. A small deer appears dancing, very cute in
                 a Disneyoid fashion.*

IGNATZ'S VOICE: A female deer . . . a doe . . .

CUT TO: *Computer-generated animation. A sine wave gradually seems to
                 be forming the shape of giant female breasts, then evolves back
                 to pure abstraction again.*

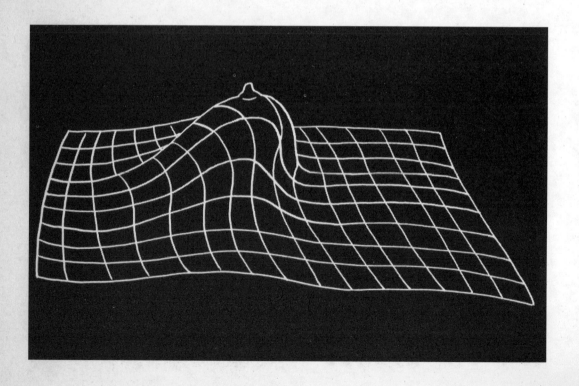

CUT TO: BETTY BOOP.

BETTY BOOP: You know, folks, you can get exactly the same effect as cocaine by shoving talcum powder up your nose, rubbing it in with sandpaper, and then running around the house burning all the money you can find.

CUT TO: *The TV studio again. The* ANNOUNCER *still confronts us with a dead-level stare, but behind him the Playmate has been replaced by the famous photo of a Vietnamese guerrilla being shot through the head on the streets of Saigon.*

ANNOUNCER: The process of rebirth can be painful and confusing. Many of the dead do not know they are dead. They think they are just wandering from room to room looking for their car keys—or watching a Cisco Kid movie about urine smugglers. Some even think they are watching educational TV.

CUT TO: IGNATZ *in pajamas, still wandering the shadowy hall. He finds a door that says* THE QUICK AND EASY PATH TO REBIRTH *and, very cautiously, opens it to peek in.*

CUT TO: *Montage of short clips:* KING KONG *peeling off* FAY WRAY's *clothes,* MARILYN CHAMBERS *registering orgasm, atomic explosions,* RONALD REAGAN *saying, "I don't remember."*

Suddenly the screen is covered with dancing red flames.

CUT TO: *TV studio again.* ANNOUNCER *now has a Crucifix on the wall behind him.*

ANNOUNCER: "And as Moses looked, the bush burned but it was not consumed. And Moses said, What is thy name? And God said unto Moses: I AM THAT I AM. Say unto the children of Israel, I AM hath sent me to you."

Echo on soundtrack: I AM . . . I AM . . . I AM . . .

CUT TO: *Long shot of typical suburban living room.* IGNATZ *and* BETTY
                 sit in easy chairs watching TV.

IGNATZ: Aw shit, Betty, not another religious show. I want some enter-
                 tainment. Isn't there a good slasher film on one of the movie
                 channels?

BETTY: Gee, Ignatz, I thought that actor looked a lot like you—the one
                 in the atom bomb sequence.

IGNATZ *ignores this and pushes a button on the remote.*

CUT TO: POPEYE *saying "I yam what I yam."*

Echo: I AM . . . I AM . . . I AM . . .

CUT TO: IGNATZ, *bored, pushes the remote switch again.*

CUT TO: J. DANFORTH QUAYLE *giving a speech.*

QUAYLE: It is a terrible waste to lose your mind . . . oh, ah, I mean not having a mind is a terrible waste. How true that is.

CUT TO: *Very unconvincing* UFOs *from THE PHANTOM PLANET.*

IGNATZ *(voice over)*: Ah, this looks like it might be good . . .

Title appears: **PLAN 3 FROM OUTER SPACE**

ALIEN VOICE #1 *(squeaky, "extraterrestrial")*: Begin interception of all Earth TV channels.

ALIEN VOICE #2: Interception of TV channels beginning 180 seconds in past time.

ALIEN VOICE #1: Recapture all past time.

ALIEN VOICE #3: All past time erased and rewritten. Nothing is.

ALIEN VOICE #2: Nothing becomes.

ALIEN VOICE #1: Nothing is not.

ALIEN VOICE #2: Rewrite past time. Activate dead brains.

ALIEN VOICE #1: Past time revised. Dead brains live.

ALIEN VOICE #2: Hail Eris.

ALIEN VOICE #3: All hail Discordia.

ALIEN VOICE #4: Let there be Slack. Keep the lasagna flying.

CUT TO: *Computer-generated fractal chaos forms. The last four speeches in reverse order.*

CUT TO: *Long shot of houses, and above, a flying lasagna.*

NARRATOR *(voice over)*: The human brain . . . this enchanted loom, as Sherrington said . . . This three-pound universe, to quote Judith Hooper . . . this hive of anarchy, as Bernard Wolfe once called it . . . this intellectual tapioca . . . It processes over ten million signals a minute.

Computer sounds as camera moves in to closeup on lasagna's convolutions.

NARRATOR (*voice over*): To duplicate your brain with state-of-the-art technology would require a computer one hundred stories high . . . and as big around as the State of Texas. And it is the last taboo organ of the body. In an age of sexual freedom, the Mind Police arrest anyone suspected of enjoying their brains.

CUT TO: *Closeup of beautiful bouquet of flowers. Camera pans back to reveal* IGNATZ *and* BETTY, *in their nightclothes, staring at the flowers, amid a lovely woodland grove.*

A POLICEMAN *appears.*

POLICEMAN: Hey, there, are you two doing something . . . *psychedelic?*

CUT TO: *Footage from Alfred Hitchcock's* SECRET AGENT. PETER LORRE *and* JOHN GIELGUD *sit at a table in a restaurant,* LORRE *enigmatic and* GIELGUD *tormented with guilt.*

LORRE (*giggling*):   So all the time you thought the universe was outside your head (*breaks down in hysterical hilarity*)... it was actually inside your head.

GIELGUD *looks half-mad with despair.*

LORRE: Inside your head. Everything you see and hear and feel—inside... (*more giggles*) chemical networks inside...

CUT TO: *Psychedelic sequence of cow on bed.*

Courtesy of the Academy Of Motion Picture Arts & Sciences

NARRATOR: Out of ten million signals a second, the brain edits out what it doesn't want, orchestrates what it does want, and creates nightmares, soap operas, ecstasies, boredom . . . a million fictions and delusions . . . If it tried to integrate all the signals at once, it would perceive only Chaos.

He is drowned out by other VOICES.

ALIEN VOICE #1: Dead brains live. Let there be Slack.

VOICE IN ECHO CHAMBER: In the third bardo, between death and rebirth, the righteous person who has burned up all bad karma shall sit with Blavatsky, Mary Baker Eddy, and Ramtha, and yea verily, they shall dine on French Canadian Bean Soup.

VOICE OF BETTY BOOP: . . . to the nearest motel for a little bouncy-bouncy . . .

ANNOUNCER: Death Of Ego . . . Death Of Ego . . . Death Of Ego . . .

VOICE OF POPEYE: Plastic imitation foreskin in frontal attack on an English author . . .

NARRATOR: Peptides act as neurotransmitters part of the time . . .

CUT TO: *A sign in a public park:*

NO DOGS IN THE PUBLIC PARK

CUT TO: *Closeup of the lasagna.*

NARRATOR *(voice over)*: This is a public service message from Outer Space about brains . . . live brains and dead brains . . . rat brains and human brains . . .

CUT TO: *Dull, listless Norway rats in cramped cages.*

CUT TO: NARRATOR, *a handsome, bearded man, walking past a yellow wall with Playmates of the Month hanging upon it.*

NARRATOR: Research shows that if you put rats in a restricted or impoverished environment, they develop mediocre brains and have low intelligence and low emotional tone.

CUT TO: *Norway rats in an enriched environment, with swings, ladders, puzzles, etc. All are happy and playful.*

NARRATOR *(voice over)*: But if you put rats from the same genetic litter in an enriched and challenging environment, they develop superior brains, with more convolutions and greater computative ability. In some cases, the brains even grow larger.

CUT TO: *Slum street in South Central Los Angeles. Gang of crack dealers stands in front of a decaying building. Caption on bottom of screen says* RESTRICTED ENVIRONMENT.

GANG LEADER: So who cares a fuck about the fuckin' rats? It's like, you know, it's one of them things, don't make a fuckin' difference. You hear me, motherfucker?

CUT TO: *Harvard student standing before ivy-covered science building. Caption tells us* ENRICHED ENVIRONMENT.

STUDENT: Yes, the rat experiments shed considerable light on the whole misguided nature-versus-nurture controversy and tend to confirm Korzybski's principle of the organism-as-a-whole-in-the-environment-as-a-whole. The holistic or synergetic paradigm fits the data in this case, certainly.

CUT TO: ANNOUNCER *in TV studio. The wall behind him now has the Communist hammer-and-sickle symbol.*

ANNOUNCER: If enough Alien Signals are thrown into the brain—enough Chaos and Confusion—the third neurological bardo prepares for rebirth on a higher level of networking. A new ego, you might say.

CUT TO: *The living room,* IGNATZ *and* BETTY *watching the TV. The* FRANKENSTEIN MONSTER *(in the corner) is reading PHILOSOPHY IN THE BEDROOM by D. A. F. de Sade.*

IGNATZ: Damn it, another educational show. Why can't I find a good slasher movie with Freddie? Or Jason? Or George Bush bombing some place?

BETTY: Wait—it might be interesting.

IGNATZ *ignores her and clicks the remote button again.*

CUT TO: ABRAHAM LINCOLN *(footage from ABE LINCOLN IN ILLINOIS) addressing a large crowd.*

LINCOLN: I'm half horse and half alligator and I wrassle tornadoes for exercise. I can eat firehouse walls and spit out the bricks, and I chew barbed wire for dental floss. I have the prettiest wife and the ugliest dawg in Illinois, and I weigh 666 pounds in zero gravity. No man can stop me, no man can top me, and I pick the goddam terror of the gods out of my nose!

CROWD *cheers.*

LINCOLN: And let me tell you this, my fine-feathered friends. French Canadian Bean Soup in one of the seven Sundays went Authoritarian in frontal attack, and it's all inside your heads. Inside your fuckin' heads, you idiots.

CUT TO: *Living room. IGNATZ and BETTY register confusion at what LINCOLN is saying.*

IGNATZ: What the hell is this shit? Did you see that commie symbol a minute ago?

He punches the remote control again.

CUT TO: *Scene from THE SIN OF HAROLD DIDDLEBOCK. HAROLD LLOYD and a lion are chained together, teetering on the ledge of a very high skyscraper. LLOYD falls and, hanging from chain, swings past a window, where he is seen by a DRUNK with a bottle. DRUNK blinks and throws the bottle away.*

LLOYD: The brain has two hemispheres, just like Jane Russell.

CUT TO: *The living room.* IGNATZ *punches the button to change channels again.*

NARRATOR *waiting to be seated in a restaurant.* WAITRESS *approaches.*

WAITRESS: Will that be smoking or nonsmoking, sir?

NARRATOR: Smoking, white, Protestant.

WAITRESS: But we can't segregate by race or religion. That would be illegal.

NARRATOR *(firmly)*: Smoking . . . white . . . Protestant. Filter tips only.

WAITRESS: But this is a democracy. We can only allow one type of segregation in each generation.

CUT TO: JULIETTE GRECO *on witness chair, from* CRACK IN THE MIRROR, *facing* ORSON WELLES.

WELLES: And what are the two hemispheres of the brain?

JULIETTE *(wiggling erotically)*: The analytical left hemisphere, called the Jane, and the intuitive right hemisphere, called the Russell.

WELLES: What are the neuropeptides that form the networks of the brain? In both hemispheres?

JULIETTE: The most important are the peptides.

She wiggles erotically and shows some leg.

WELLES: Which peptides play the crucial role?

JULIETTE: Probably the endorphins.

WELLES: I'm convinced. Come into my chamber and sit on my face for a half hour.

CUT TO: ACTOR *in tuxedo appears onstage and walks to podium. He places script on podium, carefully dons horn-rimmed glasses, and reads, in a rolling baritone, with great sincerity and poetic enunciation.*

ACTOR: There was a young lady named Gloria
                  Who got humped by Sir Geoffrey de Maurier
                  Then six other men,
                  Then Sir Geoffrey again,
                  Then the band at the Waldorf-Astoria.

He bows to polite applause from the audience.

CUT TO: *Tyrone Power as the* SINCERE SEEKER *and Sam Jaffe as the* WISE GURU *in* THE RAZOR'S EDGE.

Courtesy of the Academy Of Motion Picture Arts & Sciences

JAFFE: Government is very simple, my son. They steal your money—which is called taxation—and then they hire cops and build jails. Then they use the cops and jails to terrorize you, so they can steal more of your money, to hire more cops and build more jails, to terrorize you further, so they can steal more of your money . . .

POWER (*stunned*): But is that all?

JAFFE (*serenely*): Oh, they also use your money to hire soldiers, to conquer other countries, to steal their natural resources, so they have more money to hire more cops and more soldiers. Then with more cops and soldiers they can rob more people inside and outside the country. It's called the Protection Racket, my son.

CUT TO: *Atomic explosion in slow motion.*

Sound of computer printer as letters D O E *appear on screen.*

CUT TO: *Closeup of the brain.*

The letters D O E *remain from last scene and become* DANCE OF ENDORPHINS.

NARRATOR: Every idea, every perception, every emotion is a dance of chemicals—endorphins, other neurotransmitters, hormones—all strictly controlled by the dreaded Mind Police.

CUT TO: *The* ANNOUNCER, *with a giant American flag behind him this time, looks unpleasantly grim.*

ANNOUNCER: One more time. (*Holds up egg.*) This is your brain. (*Shows a frying pan.*) This is stupid TV commercials, repeated every day. (*Drops egg into frying pan.*) This is your brain suffering from those stupid TV commercials.

Closeup of frying egg.

ANNOUNCER: Any questions?

CUT TO: *The living room.* IGNATZ *and* BETTY *watch TV.*

IGNATZ: Hey, I don't like this—they're saying our brains are full of chemicals and the government robs from us. Is this commie propaganda?

CUT TO: *Sign in the public park:*

NO ALCOHOLIC BEVERAGES

ALLOWED IN THE PUBLIC PARK

CUT TO: *A* MIDGET *sitting in a chair in an otherwise unfurnished room.*
                   A giant photo of Marilyn Monroe hangs on one wall, King Kong
                   on another. The MIDGET *is "playing" the violin, but he only*
                   plays one note, over and over, a monotonous and eerie effect. A
                   gray-haired HOUSEWIFE *enters.*

HOUSEWIFE: Max, Max, for God's sake, Max, what is it with this one note all
                   the time? Other men who play the violin play all sorts of notes
                   and make tunes and melodies and whole sonatas even, so what
                   is it with this one note, Max, will you?

MIDGET: Those other guys are looking for the place. I found it.

CUT TO: *Back of a car in Los Angeles smog with bumper sticker saying*:

                              I FOUND IT.

NARRATOR *(voice over)*: Konrad Lorenz won the Nobel prize in 1973 for his
                   work on imprinting. An imprint is a chemical bond, a circuit in
                   the brain, that says I FOUND IT. We make our first imprint at
                   birth, an oral survival imprint that identifies a Mother or Mother
                   Substitute who will feed us.

CUT TO: *Mother image* .

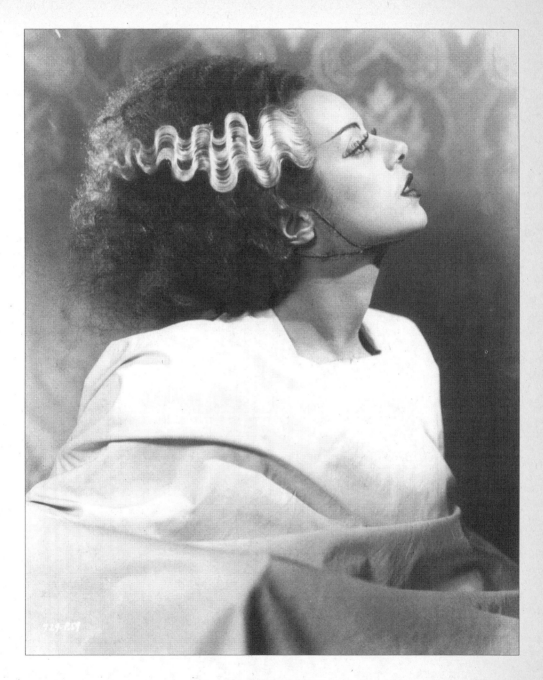

MOMMY

NARRATOR: If no Mother is present, we imprint the nearest possible Mother Substitute. Lorenz actually observed a gosling who had imprinted a Ping-Pong Ball as Mother Substitute. When we grow up, we learn to imprint green pieces of paper as oral survival tickets.

CUT TO: *Montage of quick shots: goslings following mother goose around barnyard, baby chimpanzee clinging to mother, human infant crawling toward mother, Donald Duck's Uncle Scrooge rolling ecstatically in a pile of money.*

CUT TO: NARRATOR *walking past movie screen with film clips of Jonestown massacre.*

NARRATOR: The neurochemicals triggered at imprint vulnerability make permanent networks. These networks become our reality-tunnel—the editing device by which the brain orchestrates the millions of signals it receives every minute. In terror, we re-imprint this circuit. That's how brainwashing works. Hostages often imprint and love their kidnappers, and draftees may even love the drill sergeant. When you feel helpless, anyone who feeds you becomes a Mother Substitute. A government . . . a band of terrorists . . .

CUT TO: *Our MIDGET, sitting under a tree in a woodland grove. He holds in his lap a book titled GALACTIC GUIDE TO PRIMITIVE PLANETS.*

MIDGET (*reading from book*):   "Terrorists, noun. Bands of thieves and murderers found on primitive planets with Type G suns; groups who act like governments." Hmm? *(Turns pages.)* "Governments, noun. Bands of thieves and murderers found on primitive planets with Type G suns; groups who act like terrorists."

CUT TO: *Another car in smog with bumper sticker saying:*

**DEFEND YOURSELVES!
THE GOVERNMENT IS TAKING
OVER OUR COUNTRY!**

CUT TO: *The baritone ACTOR at the podium. He reads again.*

ACTOR: There once was a monk in Iberia
             Whose existence grew drearier and drearier
             'Til he burst from his cell
             With a hell of a yell
             And eloped with a Mother Superior.

Polite applause.

CUT TO: *The living room.*

BETTY:	Somebody's fucking with our TV, Ignatz.
IGNATZ:	Our TV? Somebody's fucking with our *heads*.
BETTY:	I'll bet it's those pesky extraterrestrial cattle mutilators.

CUT TO: EXTRATERRESTRIALS *report to their* SUPERIOR.

EXTRATERRESTRIALS *(squeaky voices)*:   Hail Eris. Let there be Slack.

SUPERIOR *(consulting his script)*:   Keep the lasagna flying. All hail Discordia.

EXTRATERRESTRIALS: The signals to Earth are intercepting all TV transmissions. All past time is being replaced by Slack.

SUPERIOR *(peeking at script again)*:   Excellent. The only way to create new circuits in primate brains is by shock and confusion. Increase subliminals. Enrich the environment. Use malathion and bumper stickers.

CUT TO: *Aerial panning shot of helicopter spraying malathion on Los Angeles. Camera pans in to show* MALE EXTRATERRES- TRIAL *at controls,* FRANKENSTEIN MONSTER *sitting be- hind him reading a book called* NOT THE ALMIGHTY.

CUT TO: *Montage of quick shots: people coughing, choking, wheezing as the malathion mingles with the smog.*

CUT TO: *Long row of cars in freeway gridlock. Camera pans low to scan bumper stickers, and we read:*

REGISTER COMMUNISTS, NOT GUNS

NUKE THE GAY WHALES

NICE COMPUTERS DON'T GO DOWN

EAT THE RICH

BABY ON BOARD

U.S. OUT OF THE MIDEAST NOW

REGISTER CAPITALISTS, NOT GUNS

KLINGON ON BOARD

THERE IS NO COMPLETE THEORY OF ANYTHING

DRUNK ON BOARD

NATIONAL SOCIALIST WHITE PEOPLE'S PARTY

NO MAN'S LIFE, LIBERTY, OR PROPERTY IS SAFE
WHILE THE LEGISLATURE IS IN SESSION

ENTROPY REQUIRES NO MAINTENANCE

COCAINE-ADDICTED PIT BULL
WITH AIDS ON BOARD

U.S. OUT OF NORTH AMERICA NOW

CUT TO: RONALD REAGAN *saying "I don't remember." This clip re-*
                peats five times, each time at slower speed so his voice grows
                more slurred with each rerun.

Subtitle: REINCARNATION AND SUPERFECUNDATION

CUT TO: *Clip from* THE MALTESE FALCON. *BOGART, ASTOR,*
                   DOBBS, and GREENSTREET *stand about a table.* BOGART
                   holds lasagna.

BOGART: Shall this brain live?

GREENSTREET: Gad, sir, it is genuine Slack. I guarantee it.

DOBBS: I stole it from Dr. Frankenstein's laboratory myself. Highest-quality human brain available.

ASTOR: Bet we can't eat just one.

CUT TO: **IF GOD DIDN'T WANT US TO EAT PUSSY,
WHY DID HE MAKE IT LOOK SO MUCH LIKE A TACO?**

CUT TO: FATTEST ACTRESS *in the Western world stands before a clenched-fist symbol.*

FATTEST ACTRESS: We of the Radical Lesbian Front wish to object violently to the blatant sexism of that last joke. Pornography is murder. A boy has never wept nor dashed a thousand kim.

CUT TO: *Medium shot of police lineup.* SHELLEY McCLOWN, *in an expensive gown, stands before a blank white wall.*

NARRATOR (*offscreen*): Name?

SHELLEY: Shelley McClown.

NARRATOR: Occupation?

SHELLEY: I am a Prophet of the New Age. I come to bring America news about the Soul and the Oversoul, the Space Brothers and the Time Sisters, reincarnation and superfecundation.

NARRATOR: Superfecundation? Jesus, do you know anything about your own brain?

SHELLEY: No, not at all. *(Proudly.)* I am Metaphysical. I do not sully my mind with vulgar materialistic science.

NARRATOR: Don't call us. We'll call you.

An Iron Weight labeled 20 TONS *falls on* SHELLEY.

CUT TO: *Dinner scene from Orson Welles's THE STRANGER.* WELLES, LORETTA YOUNG, EDWARD G. ROBINSON, *and others are eating and talking.*

WELLES: And so, you see, the cat is dead and alive at the same time.

ROBINSON (*frowning*): But that's impossible, damn it!

WELLES (*witty twinkle*): Erwin Schrödinger proved it. He's got a Nobel prize in physics. He also proves you're dead and alive at the same time.

CUT TO: *Animation of* SCIENTIST *placing radioactive element in box, then adding poison gas pellet, then shoving a cat into the box and slamming the door.*

NARRATOR: Yes, Dr. Schrödinger proved that existence and nonexistence can coexist. This is Dr. Schrödinger's argument. Suppose a scientist places a radioactive element in a box, then adds a poison gas pellet, and then a cat. An element is made up of atoms, and the atoms are made up of quantum systems that act like particles part of the time. . . . But they also act like waves part of the time. . . .

      This gives the little bastards a lot of uncertainty. They are so uncertain, in fact, that physicists think they are neither particles nor waves. They only become particles or waves when we constrain them by making a measurement. When we are not making a measurement, the little buggers are in every possible state.

      Therefore, the radioactive element is in every possible state until we measure it. And the poison gas pellet is in every possible state, too, because it settles into one state only when the radioactive element settles into one state. And the cat is in every possible state, too.

Animation of cat in every possible state. Gradually, she settles down into two states, a dead cat and a live cat looking in puzzlement at the dead cat.

NARRATOR: The cat can only be in two states, practically speaking—dead or alive. But the cat remains in both of those states, until we make a measurement. And since we're all quantum systems, we're in all possible states—until we take our own measurement, as it were.

CUT TO: *Newsreel of* POPE JOHN PAUL II, *speaking to a huge crowd in Phoenix Park, Dublin.*

NARRATOR (*offscreen*): What do you think modern youth needs most, Your Holiness?

POPE (*his own words, although edited out of context*): Sex and drugs!

CUT TO: *Our baritone* ACTOR *at podium. He reads:*

ACTOR: There was a young lady named Puck
                 Who had the most terrible luck
                 She stood up in a punt (*dramatic pause, looks over his glasses*)
                 And got bit on the front
                 By a goose and a swan and a duck.

CUT TO: *The TV studio.* ANNOUNCER *now has the Islamic moon-and-
                 star symbol on the wall behind him.*

ANNOUNCER (*mumbling, seemingly stoned on downers*): The plastic imitation
                 foreskin was necessary in Poland. . . .

CUT TO: *The* APE-PEOPLE *approaching a Black Monolith.*

NARRATOR (*voice over*): Our brains, of course, are not just made of chemical
                 reactions. The chemicals are made of atoms, which are made of
                 quantum systems in every possible state . . . When the accumu-
                 lated facts and tools of neuroscience reach Critical Mass, we
                 will be able to reprogram our brains entirely and become, in
                 effect, superhuman. We will probably reach that point within
                 five years.

One APE-MAN *touches the Black Monolith and leaps back, frightened.*

APE-MAN: In *five* years?

CUT TO: BRONTOSAURUS.

BRONTOSAURUS: I don't believe all this Future Evolution crap. Things will go as
                 they always have.

CUT TO: *Living room.* FRANKENSTEIN MONSTER *has left;* WOLF
                 MAN *sits in corner, reading* HOWL *by Allen Ginsberg.*
                 IGNATZ *and* BETTY *up front in easy chairs watching TV.*

IGNATZ: See, Betty, I told you this was commie propaganda. They're
                 tryna tell us to use our brains.

BETTY (*absently*): Then six other men, then Sir Geoffrey again—Gee, I wonder
                 what that would be like.

CUT TO: *Tight closeup of* BETTY *in bed, registering erotic frenzy. Camera pans back to reveal her paramour is a distinguished English gentleman.*

Camera pans back farther to reveal, waiting by the bed, six other men, then twelve more men who all carry musical instruments.

IGNATZ *(voice over):* Betty! Control your fantasies! The whole world is watching!

CUT TO: *Medium shot of* MIDGET *and* NARRATOR *standing in a jungle, both dressed in white tropical suits.*

MIDGET: What is the New Age?

NARRATOR: The most pretentious load of Bullshit to come down the pike
                   since the Dominicans started burning witches.

BETTY *walks by in a skimpy bikini. The eyes of the* MIDGET *and the* NAR-
RATOR *mechanically turn to follow her.*

ANNOUNCER (*voice over*):   The sexual imprint is made at puberty, when the
                   neurotransmitters begin to trigger sex hormones—but that's
                   getting ahead of the story. We were talking about the oral sur-
                   vival imprint, I think. . . .

CUT TO: *Medium shot of* TAMMY FEE *on white wall background.*

TAMMY FEE: Hail Eris. All hail Discordia. Too long has the world been ruled
                   by male gods and male mortals. We of the Discordian Doubt
                   worship Eris, Goddess of Chaos, Discord, Confusion, Bureau-
                   cracy, and International Relations. Do you deny Her power?
                   Look around, and what do you see the most of? Chaos, dis-
                   cord, confusion, bureaucracy, and international relations. The
                   five levels of chaos, we call them. Simple chaos to complex
                   chaos. Who put all that disorder here, you damned atheists?

CUT TO: *The* GREEK GODS *are having a party. Aside from their Greek
                   robes, they look like Marin County yuppies.*

TAMMY FEE (*voice over*):   All our problems began with the Original Snub. The
                   gods had a party and refused to invite Our Lady Eris. Do you
                   know what She did? She made a beautiful apple of pure gold . . .

ERIS, *cackling like a witch, throws the golden apple into the midst of the party.*

TAMMY FEE (*voice over*):   Some say it was metallic gold and some say it was
                   Acapulco Gold, but be that as it may, she wrote on it Καλλιστι.

The Golden Apple. As we look, Καλλιστι fades into the English translation, TO THE PRETTIEST ONE. *The Apple glows brighter and softer, brighter and softer, in light-show effect.*

TAMMY FEE *(voice over)*: Each goddess claimed she was the prettiest one and entitled to the wonderful Apple. As a matter of fact, Hermes claimed he was the prettiest one, too—you know about Hermes. The feudin' and fightin' was something fierce, I tell you. Eventually, even mortals got dragged into the squabble, and the Trojan War resulted. The fifth state of chaos, international relations. . . .

CUT TO: GREEKS *attacking Troy.* GREEKS *creeping into a giant wooden horse.* GREEKS *climbing out of the horse to slay Trojans. One Greek looks like* PETER LORRE *and can be heard muttering over the howls and chaos of battle.*

LORRE: Inside our heads . . . it's all inside our heads.

LORRE *gets run through with a sword and dies.*

TAMMY FEE *(voice over)*: And ever since then, we've had chaos and discord and confusion and bureaucracy and international relations. And any damned atheist who doesn't believe this is going to get such lousy karma, he'll be reborn as a Jesse Jackson button and get stomped in a pool-room fight. You better accept Eris into your pineal gland before it's too late, brothers and sisters.

CUT TO: *Caption:*

DISCORDIAN SOCIETY
"ON THE SITE OF THE BEAUTIFUL FUTURE SAN ANDREAS CANYON"
LOS ANGELES   SEND MONEY   SEND MONEY   SEND MONEY

CUT TO: *The sign in the public park. It now reads:*

**NO NECKING OR PETTING
IN THE PUBLIC PARK**

CUT TO: *Long shot of* MIDGET *and* NARRATOR *standing in jungle.*

MIDGET: Would you repeat that definition of the New Age? I'm not sure
                 I got it.

NARRATOR: The New Age is the greatest evolutionary breakthrough since
                 our ancestors crawled out of the sea onto the land. It is a bio-
                 logical, technological, neurological, and psychological transfor-
                 mation unprecedented in history.

MIDGET: Wait a goddamn minute here. You just said it was a load of
                 bullshit.

NARRATOR: That's right.

MIDGET: Well, which is it?

NARRATOR: It's both. Some things called New Age are tremendous evolu-
                 tionary mutations. Other things called New Age are pure
                 bullshit.

MIDGET: Well, how can we tell the difference?

NARRATOR: The only way to distinguish the pure gold from the counterfeit
                 is . . . to learn to think for yourself. *To learn to think for your-
                 self.* Got it? To stop being robots.

BETTY *walks past in the bikini again. The eyes of the* MIDGET *and the* NAR-
RATOR *robotically follow her.*

CUT TO: *Bumper sticker:*

**IF GODDESS DIDN'T WANT US TO LICK DICK
WHY DID SHE MAKE IT SO MUCH LIKE A POPSICLE?**

CUT TO: COP.

COP: We of the Radical Masculinist Party wish to object to that last bit, which is blatant sexism. Mother is the best bet, and don't let Satan draw you into Cherry Valley by the testicles.

CUT TO: *The living room. The* WOLF MAN *is now reading a Nero Wolfe mystery.*

IGNATZ: You see? It's gotta be the commies.

BETTY: I tell ya, it's them extraterrestrial gene-splicers.

CUT TO: *Footage from* THE WOMAN IN GREEN. HILLARY BROOKE *attempting to hypnotize* SHERLOCK HOLMES.

BROOKE: You do not need cocaine any longer, Mr. Holmes. It is cocaine that keeps you addicted to Earth and prevents rebirth on a higher plane. You will lose all need for cocaine and ascend to the realm of Buddha, Ramtha, and Big Rock Candy Mountain.

HOLMES: Couldn't I do just a few lines before we go any further?

BROOKE: You do not need "a few lines." You need deep drowsy sleep . . . deep sleep . . . and you will awaken reborn as a Jesse Jackson button.

HOLMES: Just one teeny little line?

CUT TO: Tight closeup on face of J. R. "Bob" Dobbs and advertisement saying:

JEHOVAH IS AN ALIEN

AND STILL THREATENS THIS PLANET

DETAILS $1   SUB-GENIUS FOUNDATION DALLAS TEXAS

CUT TO: *Footage from the World's Worst Movie, CALTIKI, THE IM-MORTAL MONSTER. A flying saucer lands, and what looks like a heap of cheap carpets gets out. (This is supposed to be a Monster from Outer Space.)*

Voice #1:	It's hot as hell under all these carpets.
Voice #2:	Christ, I think our sneakers are showing.
Voice #3:	Any you guys got any ludes?
Voice #2:	I still think our sneakers are showing.
Voice #4:	What was that stuff about endorphins?
Voice #1:	Our brains are supposed to be made up of chemicals, I think.
Voice #5:	Fuck that. Let's send out for a pizza.
Voice #2:	No anchovies on mine.
Voice #1:	But I love anchovies . . .
Voice #3:	Hey, ain't you listening? I asked if any you guys got any fuckin' ludes?
Subtitle:	**IF VOTING COULD CHANGE THE SYSTEM IT WOULD BE ILLEGAL**
CUT TO:	NARRATOR *standing in a police lineup. Voice of* COP *offscreen.*

COP *(voice over)*: Name?

NARRATOR: Robert Anton Wilson.

COP *(voice over)*: Profession?

NARRATOR: Philosopher—or public nuisance.

NARRATOR *(voice over)*: You aren't sure?

NARRATOR: It's been a controversial question in my profession ever since Socrates.

COP *(voice over)*: The purpose of this film, if any?

NARRATOR: A Three Stooges comedy for the neurological age. An owner's guide to the human brain. A How-To Guide—how to use your brain for fun and profit.

COP *(voice over)*: Well, that settles it. You're a public nuisance.

Weight labeled 20 TONS *falls on* NARRATOR.

Subtitle: **IF NOT VOTING COULD CHANGE THE SYSTEM IT WOULD BE ILLEGAL**

CUT TO: *Footage from* THE ADVENTURES OF SHERLOCK HOLMES. *Basil Rathbone as* HOLMES *talks to* STRANGER *on ship deck.*

HOLMES: You wouldn't have a few snorts of coke you could spare?

STRANGER: Rebirth as a female deer? A dumbshit is powerful?

CUT TO: SHELLEY McCLOWN *and* MIDGET *sit in chairs facing each other but talk to audience as if this is a TV show.*

SHELLEY: Hi there, folks. This is Shelley McClown again, and I want you to meet one of the most wonderful channels I have ever met. Folks, give a big hand to Fission Chips from Liverpool, England.

MIDGET (*in correct, non-Liverpool English*):   It's great to be here with you tonight, Barbara.

SHELLEY: That's Shelley, Mr. Chips.

MIDGET (*startled*):   You're not Barbara Walters?

SHELLEY (*a bit miffed*):   No, I am *not* Barbara Walters.

MIDGET: But my agent said—I mean—ah um . . . *who* are you?

SHELLEY: I am Shelley McClown, the wisest woman in Holywood with a wicked pack of cards.

MIDGET: Oh, yes, of course, I'm dreadfully sorry.

SHELLEY: I was just about to tell the audience about your wonderful channeling.

MIDGET: Yes, I am the leading psychic in the British Isles. Some even call me the English Channel. Ha, ha. (*Coughs modestly.*)

CUT TO: *Living room.* WOLF MAN *is now reading LITTLE RED RIDING HOOD.*

BETTY (*now in her bikini*):   Well, the TV seems to be getting back to normal. Maybe it was the weather conditions in Outer Space.

Closeup of IGNATZ, now in pajamas, looking worried.

IGNATZ (*voice over*):   Detroit Orders Entropy . . . David Owsley Engleheimer . . . Dashboards On Elephants . . . Department Of Economics.

Subtitle: **D O E   D O E   D O E   D O E**

CUT TO: *The TV studio,* SHELLEY *and the* MIDGET.

SHELLEY: And how did you get such an interesting first name, Mr. Chips?

MIDGET: Oh, Fission. Well, my father was a physicist, and I was born on August 6, 1945. Hiroshima, you know.

SHELLEY: How unusual.

MIDGET: Not really. I have a friend who was born on April 19, 1942.

SHELLEY: You mean?

MIDGET: He's named D. Lysergic Acid Diethylamide Ferguson. His mother was a chemist.

SHELLEY: How baroque. But our audience is all curious, I'm sure. What Entity do you channel, Mr. Chips?

MIDGET: Gonad the Barbarian.

SHELLEY: I beg your pardon?

MIDGET: Gonad the Barbarian. He conquered the whole world in 100,000 B.C. Tops in his field—rape, pillage, murder, genocide. A sort of one-man CIA. Of course, he's become more spiritual after being dead a hundred thousand years.

SHELLEY: And how do you contact this Entity?

MIDGET: Easy as pie. Just call his name three times, and I'll go into trance and Gonad will start speaking through me.

SHELLEY: Ready, folks? Here we go. Gonad ... Gonad ... *(coaxing)* oh, Gonad ...

Closeup of MIDGET *as he sinks into a trance. His face becomes a mask of low cunning and brutality. He speaks in the voice of Arnold Schwarzenegger.*

MIDGET: I, Gonad the Great, am now with you, to speak over the magic
                     picture box. I must say you are a choice morsel, my little wench.
                     (*Leers.*) Care to drop over to the nearest motel for some bouncy-
                     bouncy?

Pan to medium shot of SHELLEY *and the* MIDGET.

SHELLEY: Uh, not really, Mr. Gonad. I thought you had become more
                     spiritual since you've been dead?

MIDGET: I intended nothing materialistic. I thought you might profit
                     from some basic lessons in Tantra yoga.

SHELLEY: Um, yes, I suppose. But tell our audience what profound secrets
                     you have learned after being dead a hundred thousand years.

MIDGET (*gradually adopting the style of Ramtha*):   Everything is everything
                     else, because all is one. . . . Good is better than evil because . . .
                     ah—because it's much nicer. Never think unkind thoughts about
                     anybody just because he's robbed you, or tried to kill you, or
                     kicked you in the balls, or anything like that. Such events are
                     your karma, and the man who does them to you is aiding your
                     future evolution. . . . High plane spirits get elected to the Col-
                     lege of Amphibology and can broadcast through channels, like
                     me. Lawyers are reborn as cabbages. Tax collectors are reborn
                     as Jesse Jackson buttons. Never smoke in the nonsmoking sec-
                     tion and never, never, never fart in church. Are you sure you
                     don't want to go to a motel and make bouncy-bouncy?

SHELLEY: Maybe a hundred thousand years isn't long enough to spiritual-
                     ize a man like you, Mr. Gonad.

MIDGET: They're not all High Church Episcopalians on the other side,
                     Barbara. You meet a lot of raunchy types—pirates, whores,
                     Holywood producers, Roman emperors. . . . I must have heard
                     every filthy limerick in the world over there. Do you know this
                     one? "There was a young man from Nantucket/Whose prong
                     was so long he could—"

SHELLEY: *Please!* This is clean family entertainment. I think in the future we better not channel anybody older than fifty thousand years.

MIDGET *(lurching out of chair)*: Enough chatter, wench. Me Gonad. Me teach you hot jungle love.

He begins to tussle with SHELLEY, *and her dress gets ripped.*

NARRATOR *(voice over)*: Before Mr. Gonad gets too unruly for the censors, let me raise the tone of the proceedings. I was saying that our first imprint—our first reality-tunnel—is an oral-survival circuit. This is basically one-dimensional.

CUT TO: *Animation: A dot moves across the screen, forming a line.*

NARRATOR *(voice over)*: One end of the line is Safe Space, or Mommy. This is imprinted orally because it's where you get fed. The other end of the line is unknown territory, possibly dangerous—a buzzing, bumpy world.

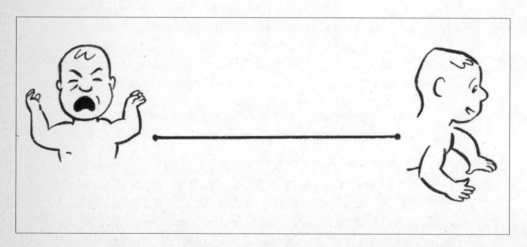

"Oh, Mommy, take me home."   *"It's fun to explore."*

NARRATOR: In this busy, bumpy world, most infants imprint the Safe Space. They want the world to be as much like Mommy as possible—and if it gets strange, they get frightened. Only a few, each generation, imprint the Explorer role. In either case, the imprint is made by neurotransmitter networks in the brain. The conservative imprints a conservative world. The innovator imprints a world of constant novelty.

CUT TO: *The sign in the public park. It now says*:

NO LOUD MUSIC

OR FUNNY CIGARETTES

IN THE PUBLIC PARK

CUT TO: NARRATOR *walking past frozen last frame of oral survival animation.*

NARRATOR: In choosing rebirth, do you want to be a frightened cabbage (*points to "take me home" face*) or do you want to be an Explorer (*points to explorer face*)? Let dead brains live. Rewrite all past time. The Sub-Genius must have Slack!

CUT TO: WELLES, ROBINSON, *and* YOUNG *having dinner.*

ROBINSON: Look, a damned cat is either dead or alive.

WELLES: But the cat is made up of atoms, which are made up of quantum systems in every possible state. So you see, old man, the cat is in every possible state.

LORETTA YOUNG: Are you talking about eigenstates or eigenvalues, honey?

ROBINSON: Too damned deep for me. Hey, did you hear the limerick about the young lady named Gloria?

WELLES: Everyone has heard that. Did you hear the one about the young man from the Coast?

CUT TO: *Helicopter dumping malathion on Los Angeles.*

CUT TO: *Bumper stickers on passing cars:*

HONK IF YOU LOVE JESUS
YOU KILLED MY BASTARD, KLINGON SON
LET JESUS INTO YOUR HEART
I AM ALSO A YOU
HONK IF YOU THINK YOU'RE TURNING INTO A GOOSE
HAPPINESS IS A WARM GUN—JOHN LENNON
HAPPINESS IS JOHN LENNON IN YOUR GUNSIGHT—MARK CHAPMAN
SUPERFECUNDATION NOW!
LET BOB INTO YOUR BANK ACCOUNT

CUT TO: *Footage from Lang's M with Peter Lorre. LORRE stands in front of mirror making lunatic faces at his own image.*

LORRE *(voice over)*: My head is inside my image of the universe ... which is inside my head ... so my head is inside my head. The Sub-Genius must have Slack?

CUT TO: *Montage of tabloid headlines:*

WORLD WAR II BOMBER FOUND ON MOON

**BABY BORN WITH EGYPTIAN BRACELET—
STUNNING PROOF OF REINCARNATION**

IRON LUNG PATIENT RAPES TWO NURSES

**MAD HUNCHBACK SELLS HUNCH TO BUTCHER:
WOMAN POISONED BY HUNCHBURGER**

**NUN'S TALE OF TERROR:
"I WAS RAPED BY MIDGETS FROM MARS!"**

CUT TO: *The living room.*

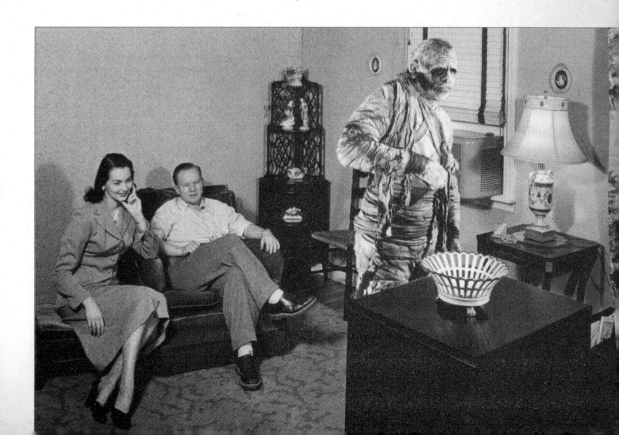

IGNATZ: The thing that bothers me is, if you're going to be an explorer, aren't you taking a chance you might get lost?

BETTY: Exactly. But I suppose, in sooth my Lord, that evolution has arranged that the majority always takes a conservative or neophobic imprint. George Bush Syndrome. But every society needs a few innovators and pioneers, so a few get the Explorer imprint every generation. Salvador Dali Syndrome.

IGNATZ: In faith, my love, you speak merrily. But that reminds me, toots, of a blind man I once knew. He had so much *chutzpah* that he took up sky-diving.

BETTY: What a ballsy guy.

IGNATZ: Yeah, but have you ever heard a German shepherd screaming for three miles down?

CUT TO: *Footage from* THE THIEF OF BAGHDAD. SABU/ELVIS *being chased by a giant* SPIDER.

Courtesy of the Academy Of Motion Picture Arts & Sciences

SABU/ELVIS: Oh, Mommy, take me home.

SPIDER: We of the Radical Feminist Caucus know the true nature of the Male Beast.

CUT TO: NARRATOR *with cigarette walking past wall decorated with Nazi war crime photos. He comes to a sign saying* THANK YOU FOR NOT SMOKING. *Searches desperately for an ash-tray. Finds none. Puts cigarette out in flower pot. Passes more Nazi photos. Comes to a sign saying* THANK YOU FOR NOT PICKING YOUR NOSE.

CUT TO: YOGI *in deep meditation, sitting in the Lotus Position.*

YOGI *(voice over):*   Oh, Mommy, take me home ... Oh, Mommy, take me home ... Oh, Mommy, take me home ...

CUT TO: *More footage from CALTIKI, THE IMMORTAL MONSTER. The* MONSTER CARPETS *are devouring a pretty young* GIRL.

VOICE #1:   I feel like a total idiot.

VOICE #4:   What the hell, the pay is good.

VOICE #2:   I think our sneakers are showing again.

VOICE #5:   I'll pay for the pizza if nobody wants anchovies on it.

VOICE #3:   Hey, save some of those ludes for me.

VOICE #2:   Have you ever been dipped in hot butter sauce?

VOICE #1:   Superfecundation, plastic imitation foreskins—I don't understand any of this.

CUT TO: *Footage from Capra's* IT'S A WONDERFUL LIFE. LIONEL
                 BARRYMORE, *as crooked banker, steals money he sees lying
                 on desk in rival's bank.*

BARRYMORE *(voice over):* Oh how money makes me hum . . . Oh how money
                 makes me hum . . . Oh how money makes me hum . . .

Subtitle: **WHO IS THE GREAT ONE WHO MAKES THE GRASS
                 GREEN?**

CUT TO: *Medium shot of garden scene.* ZEN MASTER *sits in Lotus Po-
                 sition;* MONK *approaches and bows.*

ZEN MASTER: What koan are you working on?

MONK: I am working on "Who is the Great One who makes the grass
                 green?"

ZEN MASTER: And do you have the answer?

MONK *(uncertainly):* Is it God?

ZEN MASTER: That will not do. Go back to your cell and meditate for another
                 week.

MONK: If I am not too bold, can you give me a hint?

ZEN MASTER: Certainly.

He hits the MONK *upside the head with his staff. Large Batman-style POW
appears onscreen.*

CUT TO: *Footage from ABE LINCOLN IN ILLINOIS.* ABRAHAM
                 LINCOLN *is still addressing the* CROWD.

LINCON: One nation under surveillance, with wiretaps and urine testing
                 for all.

CUT TO: POPE JOHN PAUL II *speaking in Phoenix Park, Dublin.*

NARRATOR: Many priests are now in open rebellion against the Church. What concessions do you plan to make to them, Your Holiness?

POPE (*emphatically*): Sex and drugs!

CUT TO: *Closeup of* SHELLEY McCLOWN *with hair mussed and dress torn. Camera pans back to reveal* MIDGET *being dragged away by two* COPS.

MIDGET: This outrage will not go unpunished. You shall know the Wrath of Gonad.

SHELLEY *tries to rearrange hair and straighten up as new* GUEST *arrives. He is obese and looks like Oliver Hardy.*

SHELLEY: And now, folks, a man who was actually taken to the Crab Nebula by our beloved Space Brothers.

GUEST (*taking seat*): Thank you, Barbara. It's good to be here tonight.

SHELLEY (*between teeth*): I am not Barbara Walters. I don't even look like Gilda Radner playing Baba Wawa, for Christ's sake.

GUEST: Oh, I'm sorry, Gilda. You do look a lot like Barbara Walters, you know.

SHELLEY: I am not Gilda Radner, either. She's dead, you nerd. (*She forces a smile and tries to regain her charm.*)

GUEST: You're not Gilda Radner? Well then, why do you look like Baba Wawa?

SHELLEY: Just tell us about the Space Brothers, please.

GUEST: Well, they look like dwarfs, and they're all Ralph Nader fans. They kept talking about wearing your seat belt when you drive and eating wholesome foods and never farting in church.

Terrible crashing and smashing sounds offscreen. MIDGET *breaks through the wall, rear, with the two* COPS, *bloody and battered, trying to hold on to him.*

MIDGET: My strength is as the strength of ten because my lust is pure. (*Leaps upon* SHELLEY.)

GUEST: My God, that's one of them again—the time-dwarfs from Zeta Reticuli.

CUT TO: *Two puppies approach a food tray.*

NARRATOR (*voice over*): The second imprint—the anal-territorial reality-tunnel—occurs shortly after the oral-survival imprint. You can tell the Top Dog in a litter from the Bottom Dog within a few days.

Larger puppy growls and smaller puppy slinks away, tail between legs.

CUT TO: *Schoolyard. A six-year-old* BULLY *threatens a nine-year-old* SISSY, *who runs away.* NARRATOR *enters frame.*

NARRATOR: The anal-territorial reality-tunnel has its origin in mammalian ritual. Excreting on a territory is a ritual signal that the territory has been claimed.

CUT TO: DOG *enters frame and pees on* NARRATOR.

NARRATOR (*attempting to ignore dog*): Domesticated primates—humans, that is— outline their territories by ink excretions on paper. Every national border marks a place where two gangs of domesticated primates got too exhausted to fight anymore and made a new territorial mark.

CUT TO: *Footage from Welles's* CHIMES AT MIDNIGHT. *The armies of Henry IV and the rebels rush forward into combat.*

FALSTAFF: Anybody got any ludes?

SOLDIERS: Hail Eris! All hail Discordia!

More footage from CHIMES: dead bodies in the mud. FALSTAFF running away.

CUT TO: *Footage from Sergei Eisenstein's ALEXANDER NEVSKY. The*
                 TWO ARMIES rush to destroy each other.

FIRST ARMY: Holy Russia! Long live the Tsar! Hail Eris!

SECOND ARMY: The Fatherland! Long live the Kaiser! All hail Discordia!

SOLDIER: Anybody got any ludes?

CUT TO: *Collage of photos from Vietnam War.*

NARRATOR: We all enter this reality-tunnel by age 3—and most never grow out of it. This new reality-tunnel is again formed by imprinted neurotransmitter networks in the brain. It is called Patriotism.

CUT TO: IGNATZ *wandering down the dark hall.*

VOICE *(offscreen)*: American life bomb went Authoritarian. We leap from human bodies. Fast Forward.

CUT TO: *Closeup of finger pushing "forward" button.*

CUT TO: *A new actor, the* ASSASSINATION BUFF, *lecturing. He has all the charm and sincerity of a professional TV anchorman. Behind him are front and back sketches of John Kennedy's body as observed in Parkland General Hospital in Dallas.*

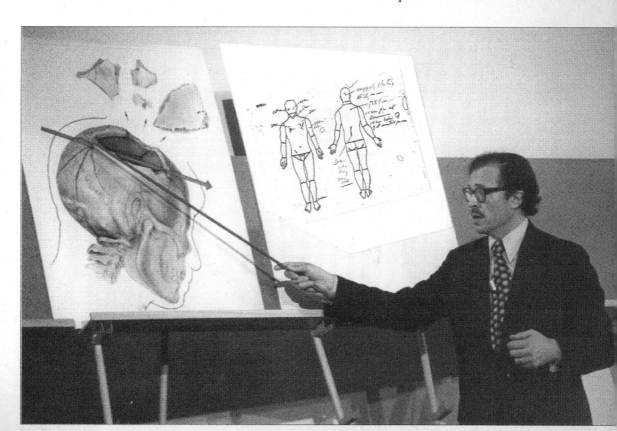

ASSASSINATION BUFF: This is the neck wound that all the doctors at Parkland
Hospital in Dallas identified as the entrance wound. (*Points to
neck.*) It looks like an entrance wound. This is the huge gaping
wound in the back of the head (*points to back of head)* that the
doctors regarded as the exit wound. It looks like an exit wound.
This is what they saw and wrote down and testified, and it
indicates the shots came from the front, from the Grassy Knoll.

CUT TO: *The crucial sequence of the Zapruder film.* KENNEDY *is hit and
his head jerks back, like any man shot from the front.*

CUT TO: *The TV studio, as before Zapruder insert. The Parkland Hospital sketches disappear and are replaced by two new sketches of
the corpse.*

ASSASSINATION BUFF: These are the sketches of what the doctors at Bethesda
Naval Hospital saw later that evening. The wound in the neck
has been enlarged, you will note, to make it look like an exit
wound. A new wound has been added in the back, between the
shoulders, which was not there at Parkland Hospital in Dallas.
Look. Do you see the changes? In making these alterations, the
whole brain disappeared. It has never been found or its absence
explained. All this was necessary to make it look as if the shots
were fired from the rear, from the School Book Depository.
Now, the Mafia couldn't do this. The pro-Castro Cubans
couldn't do it. The anti-Castro Cubans couldn't do it. No group
of rich right-wingers outside the government could do it. The
changes were made while the corpse was in the hands of government agents. And the changes were made immediately, as
soon as the corpse was put on Air Force One. Only a group
within the government could do this. And the only group in the
government with the motive and the means and a history of
arranging assassinations was the (*slow emphasis*) C . . . I . . .

Screen goes blank. Weird extraterrestrial noises. Sign appears:

DO NOT ADJUST YOUR MIND

IT IS REALITY THAT IS MALFUNCTIONING

CUT TO: NARRATOR *standing before TV Announcer set. In the background,* TWO MEN IN WHITE *are forcibly administering a hypodermic sedative to the* ASSASSINATION BUFF.

NARRATOR: We don't know how he got in . . . some wandering nut, obviously . . . He'll get the medical attention he needs.

ASSASSINATION BUFF, *sedated, zombielike, is dragged off by the* MEN IN WHITE.

CUT TO: *The unconvincing UFOs from THE PHANTOM PLANET.*

VOICE #1:   End Kennedy sequence. Rewrite past time.

VOICE #2:   Yes. We must not destroy their reality-tunnel too fast. Let there be Slack.

VOICE #3:   No goddamn anchovies, I said!

CUT TO: *A Mercator map of the world.*

NARRATOR *(voice over)*: The trajectory of human history can be stated in four simple words—Fast Westward, Fast Forward. Those with neophobic imprints—"Oh, Mommy, take me home"—stay in one place, where they were born.

A dot appears over Thailand.

NARRATOR: Those with neophilic imprints—"It's fun to explore"—keep moving Westward, against the spin of Earth, creating new ideas as they travel. Consider the order of the discovery of the chemical elements—which is one trajectory of the direction and acceleration of human progress.

Each element is represented by a dot lighting up and flashing on the map. They move steadily in an east-to-west direction.

NARRATOR: In this simulation, one minute equals six thousand years, or one hundred years per second. The first nine elements were discovered in Asia, before the birth of Christ.

We see the dots light up.

NARRATOR: Then, faster and faster, the elements were discovered in Europe, moving from southeast to northwest. The Holy Inquisition sort of killed off science in Southern Europe, as you can see.

The dots light up and cluster in Northern Europe.

NARRATOR: By 1932 we knew all the natural chemical elements. Since then we have created quite a few new elements, all of them in Southern California.

The dots move west to California in the last part of the last second.

NARRATOR: Fast Westward, Fast Forward.

CUT TO: *Medium shot:* IGNATZ *is in a grubby hippie pad, wearing Punk clothes. He has a joint in his mouth and is laying out Tarot cards for a "reading." Poster of John Lennon on wall behind him.*

AUTHORITARIAN VOICE (*offscreen*):   You think you're pretty damned smart, don't you, you insignificant little turd?

IGNATZ *looks up guiltily, awed by* AUTHORITARIAN VOICE.

AUTHORITARIAN VOICE: Oh, you know all about Tarot and the Tree of Life and how to get high on Weed. You dig the latest in art and music and film. You're fuckin' *hip*, baby. But what about the left brain? Do you know anything about that, melon head?

Camera pans around room, highlighting air conditioner and stereo as AUTHORITARIAN VOICE *drones on in tones of rebuke.*

AUTHORITARIAN VOICE: How does the Mysterious Stereo function? Why does the Mystic Air Conditioner make the air cooler? Have you ever wondered about these things? Are you using only *half* your brain power?

CUT TO: *Long shot of jet airplane taking off.*

AUTHORITARIAN VOICE (*still offscreen*): What is the Magic Art that allows a super-jet to lift 400 people off the ground and put them down safely over 4,000 miles away?

CUT TO: IGNATZ *in hippie set, looking downcast and Bottom Dog.*

CUT TO: *The brain as flying lasagna..*

AUTHORITARIAN VOICE: The long-hidden secrets of the left brain are known to High Adepts at the Princeton Institute for Advanced Studies. Now they are willing to share their mystic knowledge with nerds like you. Yes, YOU, and any other jerk like you. Now is your chance to learn about the Syllogism, which tells when an argument is sound and when it's just hot air. Or about the Equation, which predicts physical events before they happen. Or the Experiment, which shows the secrets of nature stark naked before your gaping moronic eyes. Sign up before it's too late.

CUT TO: *The living room. IGNATZ and BETTY are watching the above on TV. In the corner, NARRATOR is reading INFO-PSYCHOLOGY by Dr. Timothy Leary.*

BETTY: Gee, I wonder if this stuff is anything like yoga? I hate those bending exercises.

IGNATZ: Advanced sages . . . hidden knowledge . . . Ha! Sounds like bullshit to me.

CUT TO: *Animation: The one-dimensional line representing the oral-survival circuit has two faces at opposite ends, saying, "Oh, Mommy, take me home," and, "It's fun to explore."*

Another line grows up vertically at a right angle to this horizontal line. At the top, a face appears, saying, "I'm in charge around this habitat." At the bottom, another face appears and says, "Please tell me what to do."

CUT TO: *Quick rerun of territorial rituals on dogs, birds, and school children. Flash cuts of war scenes from CHIMES AT MIDNIGHT and ALEXANDER NEVSKY.*

NARRATOR (*voice over*): The first-circuit chemical bonds determine brain programs of conservatism or innovation. The second-circuit bonds determine programs of domination or submission.

CUT TO: *Closeup of Norway rat.*

RAT: I don't believe this chemical bond craperoo. I know I've got free will.

CUT TO: *The Mercator map, with animation.*

NARRATOR *(voice over)*: The so-called Norway rat actually originated in Southeast Asia.

A dot appears in Cambodia.

NARRATOR: This randy little rodent soon migrated west and was known in India before Buddha. At the time of Christ, *mus rattus norwegicus*—to give him his full title—was well established in the Mideast. Around 1300, he arrived in Europe, bringing bubonic plague with him, a fact that did little to increase his popularity.

Dots follow this migration across the map.

NARRATOR: In the 18th Century, he brought the plague to Norway, which has gotten blamed for him ever since. At the Continental Congress in 1776, delegates complained about the number of rats in Philadelphia. By 1859, the Norway rat was known and loathed in San Francisco. By 1872, he had arrived in Honolulu. This amazing little beast had circumnavigated most of the globe in a few thousand years.

Dots have followed this migration.

NARRATOR: Nowadays, the Norway rat is increasingly found on jet airliners. This versatile rodent will probably infest the first Space Cities within twenty years. But this cute little bugger only has a genetic program for ubiquity. Domesticated primates have also migrated all over the planet and have another genetic program, lacking in the rat. Domesticated primates like you and me have a program to create ideas—cultures—civilizations.

CUT TO: *The sign in the park, now saying:*

                         NO BICYCLES IN

                         THE PUBLIC PARK

CUT TO: ABRAHAM LINCOLN *and* CROWD

LINCOLN: And so you must learn to think for yourselves and question Authority.

HECKLER: And why the hell should we, wise guy?

LINCOLN: Because I say so, and I'm an Authority.

CUT TO: NARRATOR *walking past stills from Marx Brothers movies.*

NARRATOR *(voice over):* In an accelerating, fast-evolving universe, whoever does not change moves backward relatively. Did you ever notice that it takes only twenty years for a liberal to become a conservative, without changing a single idea?

CUT TO: *Footage from John Huston's BEAT THE DEVIL.* ROBERT MORLEY *and* UNKNOWN MAN *are trying to close an overstuffed and recalcitrant steamer trunk.* MORLEY *is arguing with* HUMPHREY BOGART..

BOGART: So everything we see is inside our heads—images made up of chemical bonds.

MORLEY: Too abstract for me. Here, push a little harder.

BOGART: Yes, yes, but listen. We have an image of ourselves inside our heads. And that image of ourselves has a head. So we have a head inside our head.

MORLEY: Have you been smoking hashish with the natives again?

CUT TO: *Half-second clip of* JANE RUSSELL *on horseback with both breasts bouncing.*

CUT TO: *Animation of the two hemispheres of the brain and their links to the right and left hands.*

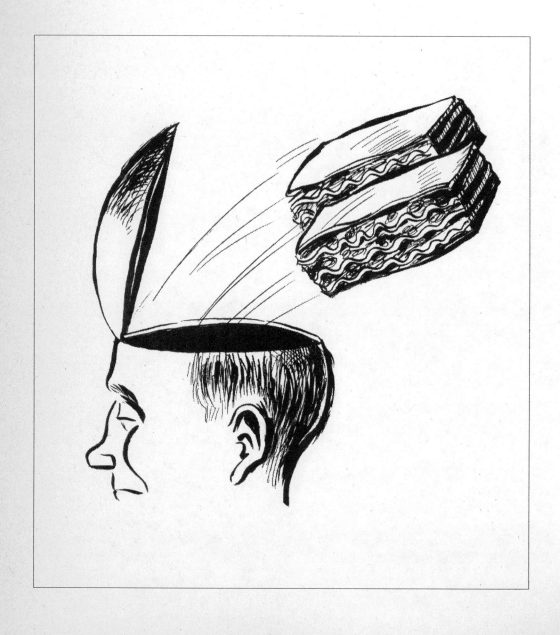

NARRATOR: Once we have an oral-survival imprint and an anal dominance-submission imprint, we are ready for the third imprint. We learn language and become part of the culture or civilization around us. We learn to manipulate things with our right hand and make maps of the universe in our left brain hemisphere.

                    Now, at last, we are in three-dimensional space. The forward-back of the oral-survival circuit criss-crosses the up-down of the anal-territorial circuit and that criss-crosses the right-left polarity of the brain itself and the hands it uses. We have advanced from oral *consciousness*—being-here-now—to anal *ego*—knowing "our place" in the primate pack—to human *mind*—making maps and models of the world.

CUT TO: *A Catholic* PRIEST. *A* LITTLE BOY *looks up at him in awe.*

PRIEST: And if you ever touch that part of your body again, you will burn in hell forever and ever and ever.

NARRATOR *(voice over)*: And if you're born in County Kerry, Ireland, the third semantic circuit imprints an Irish Catholic reality-tunnel.

CUT TO: *A* RUSSIAN, *fur cap and all, talking to the same* LITTLE BOY.

RUSSIAN: And the Capitalist Pigs then invented religion to subjugate the masses and keep them ignorant.

NARRATOR *(voice over)*: And if you're born in Moscow, the semantic circuit will imprint a Marxist reality-tunnel.

CUT TO: *The living room scene again. The* MUMMY *is reading* NEUROPOLITIQUE *by Leary, Wilson, and Koopman.*

IGNATZ: I'm gonna call the FCC and complain. First they tell us we got chemicals in our heads, and now they say we all been brainwashed. What the fuck is this?

CUT TO: *An* IRANIAN *and the* LITTLE BOY.

IRANIAN: And every page of the Koran is the word of God, so Salman
                 Rushdie has to be killed for his blasphemy.

NARRATOR (*voice over*): Or an Islamic fundamentalist reality-tunnel can get im-
                 printed. It's all mechanical, in any case.

CUT TO: *An* ENGLISHMAN *and the* LITTLE BOY.

ENGLISHMAN: So nothing is certain, but science improves a little bit with every
                 new discovery.

NARRATOR: Or an Oxford Agnostic reality-tunnel gets imprinted.

CUT TO: THUGGEE LEADER *is exhorting his followers.*

THUGGEE LEADER: Our plans are made. Our recruits are ready. The astrological
                 omens are correct. Jupiter is in trine with Mars and the Black
                 Monolith is in quinine with Venus. Jupiter is in the third house,
                 Pluto is in the outhouse, and Mercury is in a whorehouse. Now
                 we will launch a frontal attack on an English author.

Closeup of CARY GRANT *eavesdropping. Registers shock and anger.*

CUT TO: NARRATOR *walks past a white screen carrying a can of film.*

NARRATOR: The funny thing about this movie business is that every single
                 frame is static. A still photo. Look.

Holds up a frame. In closeup we see a shot from a CISCO KID *sequence.*

NARRATOR: We all know this, but if I put the film in a projector . . .

*He puts the film in a projector. On the blank screen th*e CISCO KID *appears in
motion.*

NARRATOR: We know it's all static frames, but we still see motion. Isn't that
                 strange, when you think of it?

CUT TO: *Footage of* MING THE MERCILESS *and* FLASH GOR-
               DON.

MING (*with Gay intonation, camping*):   At last we're in a film with real philo-
               sophical depth . . . Maybe I can explain the great Tao to you at
               last . . .

FLASH (*Clint Eastwood's voice*):   Never mind that, you evil old fart. I know Dow
               personally, and Jones, too. I want to ask you about interplan-
               etary urine smuggling.

MING (*with a campy flash of anger*):   We will make you regret asking that ques-
               tion. You will be locked in a closed Murphy bed for forty days
               and forty nights with a Liverpool Punk group who haven't
               washed since Saint Tibb's Day.

FLASH: Oh, blow it out of your ass, wise guy.

CUT TO: *Long shot of a laboratory. A distinguished elderly* SCIENTIST
               stands behind a long table, wearing a white lab smock..

A banner across the front of the table proclaims:

COMMITTEE FOR SLANDER, INVECTIVE, AND CALUMNY AGAINST OPEN-MINDED PEOPLE (CSICOP)

The CSICOP SCIENTIST *begins a doddering speech.*

CSICOP SCIENTIST: After painstaking scientific investigation, we have concluded that there are no alien spaceships around here, and anybody who disagrees with us is a nameless asshole. Ordinary people, who are not Experts like us, simply do not know what they are looking at most of the time. They do not have the Infallibility of true Authorities like the members of this committee. They are subject to confusion and delusion and muddled thinking.

CUT TO: *UFOs destroying the Capitol, the White House, the Eiffel Tower, etc.*

CSICOP Scientist (*voice over*): Some UFO reports are hoaxes. Some are hallucinations. When two people see it, that's dual hallucination. When hundreds see it, that's mass hallucination.

UFOs continue to wreak havoc on Earth.

CUT TO: *UFOs flying in formation.*

Voice #1:   One of the experimental subjects is calling the FCC to complain about us.

Voice #2:   Thank Goddess our agents on Earth continue to insist we're not here.

Voice #3:   They all get a faraway look in their eyes. It's Chinatown, Jake.

Voice #4:   No anchovies with plastic imitation cow piss.

CUT TO: BELA LUGOSI *emerging from a mausoleum.*

Lugosi: After forty years on junk, I finally quit. The next week I died and they put me here. What an advertisement for rehabilitation.

CUT TO: *More UFOs with dubbed dialogue (still squeaky and "extraterrestrial").*

Voice #1:   A very primitive and paranoid age, as Admiral James T. Kirk warned us.

Voice #2:   Pancho, once a humble sidekick, has become as rich as the Pope.

Narrator (*voice over*): Remember what we just showed you? Nothing is moving. It's all single frames.

Picture freezes.

Narrator: As Plato said, Time and Motion, which are serial, are the moving images of Eternity, which is One.

CUT TO: *Medium shot of the* FATTEST ACTRESS *in the world.*

FATTEST ACTRESS: We of the Lesbian Radical Caucus Revolutionary Task Force
                     know the true nature of the Male Beast. All sexual intercourse
                     with men is humiliating and painful, unless the man doesn't
                     have an erection.

CUT TO: *Footage from* PLAN 9 FROM OUTER SPACE. A CHIRO-
                     PRACTOR, *pretending to be Bela Lugosi holding a cape in
                     front of his face, creeps furtively toward house.*

The HOUSEWIFE *rises in terror. The* CHIROPRACTOR *advances.*

CHIROPRACTOR: It's okay, I don't have an erection.

HOUSEWIFE *flees out the door and runs into* BASIL RATHBONE *as* SHERLOCK HOLMES.

HOLMES: I was wondering if I could borrow some sugar . . . and maybe a few lines of coke.

CUT TO: *More bumper stickers on cars:*

CAMPUS CRUSADE FOR CHRIST
CAMPUS CRUSADE FOR CTHULHU
HONK IF YOU LOVE HONKING

GOD SPELLED BACKWARDS IS DOG
BUT BOB SPELLED BACKWARDS IS STILL BOB
THERE WAS A YOUNG MAN FROM THE COAST?

R Douglas Smith

CUT TO: PREACHER *in pulpit.*

PREACHER: And don't you believe these New Age Satanists and Swamis
                and their Space Brothers. These aliens in flying saucers don't
                mean us any good at all, and Our Lord has told us so—right
                here last week, when he channeled to us through that wonderful
                little man from Liverpool, Fission Chips. Jesus himself said,
                speaking through our little brother Mr. Chips, that these aliens
                from the Crab Nebula are in league with the Intergalactic Bank-
                ers and the Illuminati.

Caption: SEND MONEY   SEND MONEY   SEND MONEY

NARRATOR *(voice over, somberly)*:   In advanced cases, if the Javafarian Coffee
                Ceremony doesn't work, I recommend a Discordian ritual called
                the Toad Elevating Moment. Eat a live toad as soon as you get
                up, and Our Lady Eris will guarantee that nothing worse will
                happen to you all day.

CUT TO: IGNATZ *with new, sleek hairdo and lab smock sitting at a
                computer, working.*

AUTHORITARIAN VOICE *(offscreen)*:   You think you're pretty damned smart, don't
                you, Mr. Wise Guy Know-It-All?

IGNATZ *cringes at the* VOICE OF AUTHORITY.

AUTHORITARIAN VOICE: Oh, you're a goddamn champ at all those linear, analyti-
                cal left-brain functions. We all know that. But what about the
                right brain, you pathetic little fuck-up? You wouldn't want to
                live with one testicle, would you? Then why try to live with
                one half of your brain, you silly wimp?
                   Nine out of ten people who try the right hemisphere are de-
                lighted with the results. Perfectly safe if used as directed by the
                Manufacturer.

CUT TO: *Footage of* JOSEPH COTTEN *and* ORSON WELLES *riding the Ferris wheel from* THE THIRD MAN.

Courtesy of the Academy Of Motion Picture Arts & Sciences

COTTEN: But if the cat is dead in one universe and alive in another, there must be zillions and zillions of universes.

WELLES (*urbane and charming*): Oh, I get so tired explaining this. Wouldn't you rather hear the limerick about the young man from the Coast?

COTTEN (*accusingly*): This is a serious matter of quantum epistemology, dammit! Don't drag everything into the gutter.

WELLES (*tracing a heart on the window pane*): "There was a young man from the Coast/Who received a strange box in the post—"

COTTEN: Stop that and be serious. And by the way, what the fuck happened to your moustache?

WELLES: I only have a moustache in half the universes where I appear— like the cat, who is only dead in half the universes.

Subtitle: **EXISTENCE AND NONEXISTENCE ARE THE SAME**
                                                                    —BUDDHA

CUT TO: CISCO KID *captured by* VILLAIN *on rocky mountain*.

CISCO KID (*with Charlie Chan accent*): We no like cattle rustlers around these parts.

VILLAIN (*with voice of Bugs Bunny*): I wasn't trying to steal the damned cows—I only wanted the cow piss.

CISCO KID: Ha! Telling that story to Marines.

VILLAIN: No, really, there's big bucks in the urine business these days.

CUT TO: NARRATOR *and* BOGART *walking in fog.*

NARRATOR: I don't get that cow-piss shit.

BOGART: I just want to hear the end of that one about the young man from the Coast.

Subtitle: **BEYOND THE CRAB NEBULA**

CUT TO: *Our poetry-reading* ACTOR *in tuxedo at podium. He turns a page, pauses dramatically, and reads with deep feeling:*

ACTOR: They are not long, the weeping and the laughter,
Love and desire and hate
I think they are no part of us, after
We pass the Gate.
They are not long, the days of wine and roses:
Out of a misty dream
Our path emerges for a while, then closes
Within a dream.

Boos, hisses, catcalls. IGNATZ *climbs onstage and hits* ACTOR *with a pie.*

CUT TO: MARIA OUSPENSKAYA *and* THE WOLF MAN.

MARIA: You must jump from the dark, like a terrorist, to launch an unprovoked attack on language and thought, then slink back to hide behind a belly laugh.

THE WOLF MAN *stumbles from the room, destroyed.*

CUT TO: INDIANA JONES *and* NARRATOR *are having one hell of a*
                 fight on a moving truck.

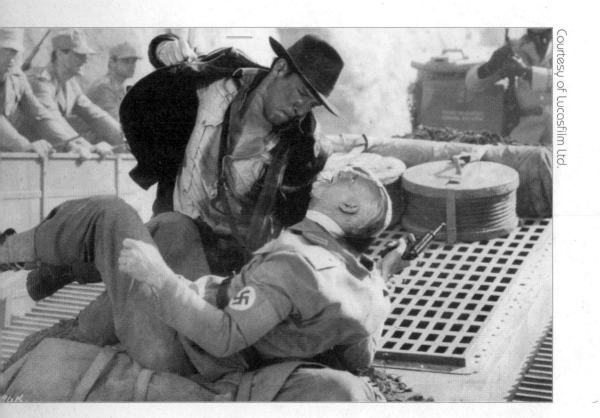

Courtesy of Lucasfilm Ltd.

JONES: Did you know that the National Science Institute isn't using
                 rats in experiments anymore? They substituted lawyers.

NARRATOR: Really? Why they do that?

JONES: Four reasons. One, animal rights activists don't give a fuck
                 what happens to lawyers. Two, there are more lawyers than rats
                 in Washington. Three, lab technicians (*pant, groan—he is*
                 knocked sprawling) don't develop emotional attachments to
                 lawyers.

NARRATOR: And the fourth reason?

JONES: There are some things you can't get a rat to do.

CUT TO: *Footage from RAIN MAN. DUSTIN HOFFMAN and TOM CRUISE are arguing in an airport.*

HOFFMAN: You don't understand. Listen again. There's a barber in Dublin who shaves every man who doesn't shave himself. Does he shave himself?

CRUISE: Well, he has to, since he doesn't . . . I mean he can't because . . . I mean . . . Is this an unprovoked attack on thought and language?

CUT TO: *Footage from HUNCHBACK OF NOTRE DAME. Angry MOB surging forward toward the Cathedral of Notre Dame.*

Courtesy of the Academy Of Motion Picture Arts & Sciences

FIRST MOB VOICE: We just want to talk to you about the Last Days.

SECOND MOB VOICE: Just open the door and we'll give you a free copy of *Awake.*

Medium shot of LON CHANEY, SR., *hopping around on the roof.*

CHANEY (*Voice of Michael Caine as Cockney*): I don't want your damned Jehovah's Witness propaganda. I belong to the Discordian Society and accepted Eris into my pineal gland five years ago.

Long shot of the MOB *with battering ram, smashing door of church.*

MOB VOICES: You need Jehovah in your life. . . . Millions now living will never die. . . . Fuck the Pope.

CHANEY *pours hot lead down on them.*

CHANEY: Hail Eris. All hail Discordia.

CUT TO: SHELLEY McCLOWN *who has freshened up.* MIDGET *has been removed, and she is interviewing the fat* GUEST *again.*

SHELLEY: And what was it like when you got to the Crab Nebula?

GUEST: It was pretty scary. The Crabs wanted to eat me.

SHELLEY: You must have been terrified.

GUEST: You can say that again. Have you ever been dipped in hot butter sauce?

SHELLEY: It sounds awful.

GUEST: Not as bad as fifty zillion light-years on the spaceship with those sanctimonious Space Brothers preaching about wheat germ and ecology and natural foods all the way.

Terrific crash and the MIDGET *breaks through wall again.*

MIDGET: Gonad shall take his bride!

CUT TO: OSTEOPATH IN GORILLA SUIT *on pulpit*.

OSTEOPATH IN GORILLA SUIT: Our Lady Eris has ordained that all things in the
                 universe shall be related to the number five, given enough inge-
                 nuity on the part of the interpreter. For instance, you have five
                 fingers. Take off your shoes, and you'll see you have five toes,
                 too. The work-week has five days; then we are granted two
                 days free of slavery. The Pentagon has five sides and is entirely
                 devoted to Our Lady's Five-Fold Plan of Chaos, Discord, Con-
                 fusion, Bureaucracy, and International Relations. The great pyra-
                 mid of Cheops has five sides, too, if you count the bottom.

CUT TO: *Fast forward.*

CUT TO: NARRATOR *sitting behind desk (Sacred Chao on wall behind
                 him).*

NARRATOR: According to J. R. Platt of Michigan State University, speed of
                 travel has increased a thousandfold since 1900. Wherever you
                 want to go, you can get there a thousand times faster than
                 Grandpa could.

CUT TO: *A MALE ACTOR who does not appear in any other scene. He stands before a white wall and very quickly makes the Four Signs of a Master Mason. This goes by so fast that most people won't know what they saw, but Masons will be startled.*

CUT TO: *Rerun of* CISCO KID, JANE RUSSELL, IGNATZ *as hippie,* WELLES *on the Ferris wheel, plus pre-runs of* HITLER *at Nuremberg,* HARPO MARX *chasing a turkey, and other bits to come—all so fast the audience can just barely register the images.*

Crash sound and numbers appear on screen, as if film broke in projector. Numbers fade to white empty screen. Pause. Just as audience begins to rumble we

CUT TO: NARRATOR *in closeup talking directly to camera.*

NARRATOR: We are about to give away one hundred million dollars—maybe. Yes, sir, I said ONE HUNDRED MILLION DOLLARS. And here's all you have to do to be a winner. After the show send us a postcard, to Gold and Apple Productions, Holywood, if, AND ONLY IF, you think most people who see the film won't bother to send a postcard. Got it? Send the card only if you think most people won't. If we get less than a hundred cards, each of you who sent one will get ONE MILLION DOLLARS. But if we get more than a hundred cards, nobody wins anything. Got it nice and clear now? *Only* send the card if you're convinced most people won't. You might win Big Bucks, my friends.

CUT TO: *The living room. The* CREATURE FROM THE BLACK
                  LAGOON *sits in the corner reading JAWS.* IGNATZ *is on the*
                  phone.

IGNATZ: Commie propaganda and all sorts of crap about chemicals in
                  our heads . . .

BETTY: Wait a minute, honey. It's just a complicated game show. We
                  might win a pile of money.

IGNATZ *slowly lowers the phone.*

CUT TO: TYRANNOSAURUS.

TYRANNOSAURUS: How much of this is real and how much is a put-on? How much of your life is real and how much is a put-on? Is George Bush real or a put-on? Is urine testing real or a put-on?

CUT TO: STAGS *in combat.*

NARRATOR *(voice over):* Of course, after we have an oral-survival circuit or "consciousness" and an anal-territorial circuit or "ego," and a semantic circuit or "mind," we are still not adults. At puberty, the DNA master-tape sends out messenger RNA molecules, and we mutate again—bodily, neurologically, mentally. We develop a Sex Role, or fourth reality-tunnel.

CUT TO: BOY *and* GIRL *walking on street, holding hands.*

CUT TO: *Personal ad from sleazo tabloid:*

YOU MISERABLE WORM! Crawl to the phone and call

Mistress Birch for the discipline you deserve.

Los Angeles 333-6666.

CUT TO: *Two* GAY MEN *walking on street, holding hands.*

NARRATOR *(voice over):* Of course, at the critical moments of imprint vulnerability, we can imprint almost any sexual reality-tunnel. We each have our own peculiar sex imprint. As the Quaker said to his wife, "All the world is a bit queer except thee and me, and sometimes I wonder about thee."

   All these chemical imprints—on the oral circuit, the status circuit, the semantic reasoning circuit, and the sex circuit— make up the programming of the robots we are pleased to call our "selves."

CUT TO: *Closeup of* SHELLEY McCLOWN.

SHELLEY: How disgustingly materialistic. Our selves are actually created by all our past incarnations, from Atlantis to the present.

CUT TO: *Fast forward.*

CUT TO: NARRATOR *walking past collage of photos of Picasso paintings.*

NARRATOR: According to J. R. Platt of Michigan State University, speed of communication has increased ten million times since 1900. Any message you want to send can travel ten million times faster than a message from Grandad in 1900.

CUT TO: *Cellar with isolation tank.* ELDERLY ENTOMOLOGIST *climbs in.*

NARRATOR: The isolation tank—now available in most American cities—sets off a train of brainwave changes.

Electro-encephalogram chart comes out of machine. We see brainwaves change.

NARRATOR: The fast, choppy beta waves of normal, outward consciousness give way to the slower, smoother alpha and theta waves. This produces a rush of new peptides, especially endorphins.

CUT TO: *Diagram of brain, with peptides rushing around forming new networks.*

NARRATOR: New networks take the form of new thoughts—new percep-
               tions. A whole new reality-tunnel can form.

CUT TO: *Diagram of human body, with neuropeptides moving through
               blood and lymph, etc., to boost immunological system.*

NARRATOR: These chemicals also feed the pleasure centers and boost the
               immune system. Many new brain-stimulating machines pro-
               duce similar results. We are robots who are learning how to
               cease to be robots.

CUT TO: MIDGET *as professor lecturing a class.*

MIDGET: Quoting Platt of Michigan State again, the destructive power of
               weaponry has increased ten–millionfold since 1900. According
               to Buckminster Fuller, half the scientists alive are working on
               weapons research—how to deliver more and more explosive
               power over longer and longer distances in shorter and shorter
               times to kill more and more people. If we don't have a New
               Age soon, we might not live to have an old age.

CUT TO: *Atomic blast and caption* DEATH OF EARTH

CUT TO: *The cock-eyed room designed by psychologist Albert Ames. NARRATOR and MIDGET enter through door and walk to opposite ends of room. NARRATOR seems to shrink to a dwarf and MIDGET swells to a giant.*

NARRATOR: There is no camera trickery in this shot. The human eye would have seen just what the camera saw. The room was designed by a master psychologist, Albert Ames, to illustrate how the brain interprets what the eyes see.

NARRATOR *and* MIDGET *walk toward each other and become their "normal" sizes.*

Subtitle: **REALITY**

CUT TO: *The* MAD BARON, FAY WRAY, *and* JOEL McCREA..

Footage from THE MOST DANGEROUS GAME. The MAD BARON *has just explained to* FAY *and* JOEL *that he intends to set them loose on his island and hunt them like animals.*

Courtesy of the Academy Of Motion Picture Arts & Sciences

MAD BARON: So therefore the barber does *not* shave himself.

JOEL: But dammit, somebody has to shave him—and he shaves every-
                  body that doesn't shave himself.

MAD BARON (*with the serene certitude of paranoia*):   So it would seem to infe-
                  rior minds, not trained as I am in Pure Logic.

FAY: Jesus, can't we send out for some Chinese food or something? I
                  don't give a fuck who shaves the damned barber.

JOEL: I tell you you are mad, Baron. Any man who doesn't shave
                  himself must be shaved by the barber.

FAY: Well, if you're not up for Chinese, how about Colonel Sanders?

Subtitle: **THE PLASTIC IMITATION FORESKIN**

NARRATOR (*voice over*): You can't understand the films of Roman Polanski until
                  you understand why he invented the plastic imitation foreskin.

Subtitle: **REALITY IS**

CUT TO: *The woodland scene.* MIDGET *looks up from a book.*

MIDGET: Did he say a plastic imitation foreskin? What was that business
                  about interstellar bankers and interplanetary urine smugglers?
                  What kinda movie is this?

Subtitle: **REALITY IS WHAT**

CUT TO: *More footage from THE CRAWLING TERROR. Ominous music as the huge carpet invades a dance hall and creates panic.*

WOMAN: Jesus fucking Christ, twenty college boys so looped on drugs they're running around under a buncha carpets!

MAN: Don't be afraid, honey, they're too spaced out to be dangerous.

Carpet devours woman.

MAN: Hey, you guys, that ain't funny. Let her go or I'll call the fuzz.

WOMAN *(inside carpet)*: Hey, you nerd, keep your hands to yourself.

The students' VOICES from inside the carpet:

VOICE #1:   Hey, gimme some of them ludes. This is getting to be fun.

VOICE #2:   Okay, we're agreed now—anchovies on one-fourth, pepperoni on one-fourth, and salami on one-third.

VOICE #3:   That leaves one-eleventh of the pizza with nothing on it.

VOICE #4:   Gimme back them ludes, you bastard.

VOICE #3:   No, really, add it up. We got eleven-twelfths of a pizza . . .

CUT TO: *Bumper stickers on cars:*

SAY NO TO DRUGS
SAY NO TO GEORGE BUSH

CUT TO: MIDGET *sitting on the edge of a Beverly Hills pool.*

MIDGET: The plastic imitation foreskin was necessary in Poland in 1944. Polanski, like many other Jewish children, was given shelter by a Catholic family after his parents were arrested by the Nazis. This family, small farmers, pretended the boy was their own to protect him from the Gestapo.

NARRATOR *(voice over):* The Nazis, of course, knew that some Jewish children were being protected this way. So they occasionally ran check-outs.

MIDGET: A Gestapo team would sweep through a village, grabbing all the little boys. They would pull their pants down. The boys with foreskins were considered Gentile and spared. The boys without foreskins were considered Jewish and sent to the Death Camps.

Subtitle: **REALITY IS WHAT YOU CAN GET**

CUT TO: *Oswiencim Concentration Camp.*

NARRATOR *(voice over)*:   Polanski survived by inventing the plastic imitation foreskin. He "passed" as a goy.

CUT TO: *The living room.* THE FRANKENSTEIN MONSTER *is reading* THE PRINCE *by Machiavelli.* IGNATZ *and* BETTY *watch TV.*

IGNATZ: Jesus, foreskins now. A while ago it was some cow-piss shit.

CUT TO: NARRATOR *in last scene from* CHINATOWN.

Courtesy of the Academy Of Motion Picture Arts & Sciences

NARRATOR: Polanski's films are set in an insane universe where life or death hinges on something as absurd as a plastic imitation foreskin.

Caption: FOR THE *CAHIERS DE CINEMA* CROWD.

NARRATOR: Orson Welles, on the other hand, observed in Beverly Hills in 1942 that you can tell when your guests are peeing in your pool. Orson said they all get a faraway look in their eyes.

He passes photo of Welles as KANE.

Subtitle: **REALITY IS WHAT YOU CAN GET AWAY WITH**

CUT TO: NARRATOR *walking past stills from Buster Keaton films.*

NARRATOR *(pausing to light cigarette)*: Chinatown is a symbol of the place where no matter what you do, things turn out wrong.

CUT TO: *The* MIDGET *by the pool.*

MIDGET: · Chinatown is like a Three Stooges film where the projector gets stuck and you keep seeing the same sadistic sequence over and over: Moe sticking his finger in Curly's eye. Over and over, forever. If you ever had Bad Acid, you know what I mean.

NARRATOR *joins* MIDGET.

NARRATOR: Polanski went to Chinatown three times. When his parents were killed by the Nazis. When his wife was killed by the Manson family. And when he got convicted of statutory rape. We all go to Chinatown, sooner or later.

NARRATOR *puts cigarette lighter down on bar stool. Camera pans in to close-up and we see lighter has the shape of the Black Monolith from 2001. Camera moves even closer and we read, at the bottom of the Monolith, the word* ROSEBUD.

CUT TO: *Rerun of psychedelic sequence of the cow on the bed.*

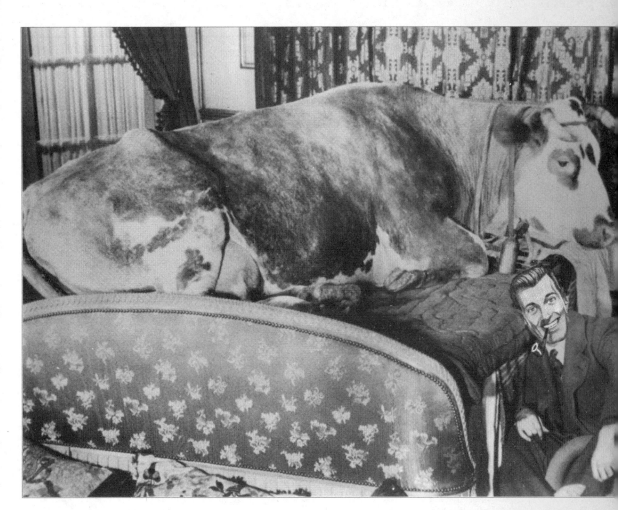

VOICES *in echo chamber:*

VOICE #1:   If the barber shaves himself, he doesn't shave himself.

VOICE #2:   . . . . so Salman Rushdie must die.

CUT TO: *A standard psychiatrist's office. The* PSYCHIATRIST *holds a pad and pencil.* IGNATZ *lies on the couch.*

PSYCHIATRIST: It was wise of you to come for therapy at this point.

IGNATZ: Jeez, I had to. It just got to the point where I couldn't tell anymore what was TV and what was reality.

PSYCHIATRIST: Well, let's just do a spot check, to see how serious the problem is. Okay?

IGNATZ (*nervously*): Okay. . . .

PSYCHIATRIST: Ronald Reagan. Real or TV?

IGNATZ: Oh, that's easy. TV.

PSYCHIATRIST: Are you sure?

IGNATZ: You bet your bippy. He's Errol Flynn's sidekick in the morning movie. He's the sheriff in the afternoon movie. In the evening, he's an Unindicted Co-Conspirator on the news.

PSYCHIATRIST: Nuclear war?

IGNATZ: Only on TV—so far.

Pan to closeup on IGNATZ, *sweating and nervous.*

PSYCHIATRIST: Death Of Earth?

Long shot. IGNATZ *turns to stare at* PSYCHIATRIST, *who is no longer in the chair. He has been replaced by a giant Norway rat.*

IGNATZ *bolts from the room.*

CUT TO: NARRATOR *in conference room, sitting behind desk.*

NARRATOR: Von Neumann gave us another way to look at the Schrödinger's cat puzzle. He suggested that the universe contains a maybe state, in between yes and no. Like this.

He tosses a coin in the air. Film freezes on immobile frame of coin in midair.

NARRATOR: Now the coin is in the maybe state.

Film moves again, and coin lands. We pan back to see NARRATOR again.

NARRATOR: Now the coin is in an either/or state again—either heads or tails. (*Looks.*) In this case, tails. But things can stay in the maybe state for a few seconds, or many centuries, or forever.

CUT TO: *Animation: Cat in the box. This time she splits into three cats, labeled* DEAD, ALIVE, *and* MAYBE.

CUT TO: ORSON WELLES *and* JOSEPH COTTEN.

COTTEN: But you can't leave me in uncertainty forever. Is the cat really dead or alive?

WELLES *(with his special sinister charm)*: Don't take it so seriously, old man. Remember the young man from the Coast, who received a strange box in the post. Inside was a bird, a pearl, and a turd, of the Duke of Windsor, on toast. *(Cryptic smile and quick exit.)*

CUT TO: HUMPHREY BOGART, ELISHA COOK, JR., *and* NARRATOR.

Footage from THE MALTESE FALCON. BOGART's first interview with Greenstreet and Cook. NARRATOR is edited in to replace Greenstreet.

BOGART *(with Peter Lorre's voice):* Well, how much is this Slack stuff worth?

NARRATOR *(Greenstreet's voice and words):* The price, sir, is inconceivable.

BOGART *(Lorre voice):* This isn't more of that cow-piss shit, is it?

NARRATOR: Do you take me for Ming the Merciless or some common urine smuggler? This is genuine Slack we are discussing.

COOK: When are we gonna send out for pizza? I want anchovies on mine.

BOGART *(sudden flare of anger):* God damn it, I told you guys I never take anchovies on my pizza. NO FUCKIN' ANCHOVIES, I said. *(He turns to stomp out of the room. As he goes:)* Cut me out of the deal if you gotta have anchovies. *(Slams door.)*

CUT TO: *Interview room, with dim light to hide the identity of the person being interviewed, a* PHRENOLOGIST *speaking in a low, tense voice.* ANNOUNCER *is interviewing him.*

ANNOUNCER: And how did you get into the urine business?

PHRENOLOGIST *(ashamed):* I was broke—I needed bread . . . and Reagan kept saying he was going to do wonderful things for small business. I suddenly flashed that, like, he was giving me a signal. I could be an entrepreneur—little old me.

ANNOUNCER: You realized there would be a market for drug-free urine, is that it?

PHRENOLOGIST: Well, hell, it stands to reason, doesn't it? I could be servicing an already existing market and hauling in the long green. Isn't that what Free Enterprise is all about?

ANNOUNCER: But our researchers have noted that your facility is in Boulder, Colorado. That's rather hard to understand. How do you manage to find any drug-free urine in Boulder, or anywhere within a hundred miles of there?

PHRENOLOGIST: We . . . ah . . . um . . . we found—ah—five people in Longmount who don't turn on.

ANNOUNCER: Five people? But you're selling hundreds of gallons of drug-free urine. You couldn't do that with five people, or even five elephants.

PHRENOLOGIST: I—um . . . what is this, anyway? Ambush Journalism? You think you're Mike Wallace or something?

ANNOUNCER: According to our researchers, you own a ranch with several thousand head of Black Angus cattle.

PHRENOLOGIST (*quickly*): The cattle are a sideline.

ANNOUNCER: We have studied your advertisements carefully. They all say quite clearly that you are selling Guaranteed Drug-Free Urine, but nowhere do they say Guaranteed Drug Free HUMAN Urine.

PHRENOLOGIST: I—I—I—

ANNOUNCER: Quite candidly, sir, are you selling cow piss through the mail and making a fortune out of it?

PHRENOLOGIST: I don't have to put up with this crap. You'll hear from my lawyer, wise guy. *(Exits.)*

ANNOUNCER: We wish to thank the Cisco Kid for his help in uncovering the vast cattle-urine-smuggling rings in the Four Corners region.

CUT TO: *Footage from the Nazi propaganda film, TRIUMPH OF THE WILL. A Nazi rally in Nuremberg, 1936.*

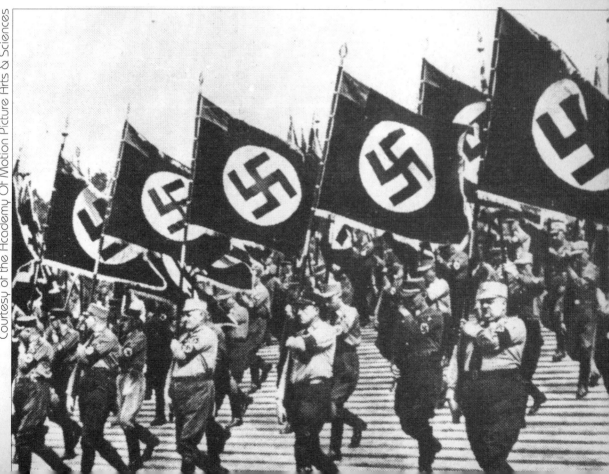

NAZI #1:   Say, Fritz, is this the Scientology Convention?

NAZI #2:   No, you dumb asshole, this is the Free Lyndon LaRouche Pro-test March.

NAZI #3:   They put anchovies on my pizza. I told you I didn't want no fuckin' anchovies.

NAZI #4:   I see Ronnie, but where's Nancy?

NAZI #5:   If this is the Jewish Defense League, who are all those guys in funny uniforms?

DAN QUAYLE *appears on the podium.*

QUAYLE: I just had my first blow-job today.

CROWD *roars, cheers, makes Nazi salutes, etc.*

QUAYLE: And even after three Margaritas I still can't get the taste out of my mouth.

CROWD *standing to repeat Nazi salute over and over, chanting "EM–EYE–SEE–KAY–EEE–WHY—EM–OH–YOU–ESS–EEE!"*

CUT TO: *A long hall with a crowd of* OFFICE WORKERS *lining up to get bottles marked "Urine Sample." Camera pans in on* IGNATZ, *grinning, and pans down to his hand inside coat holding bottle marked "GUARANTEED DRUG–FREE URINE."*

We pan back to the longest goddamn tracking shot in the history of films as thousands and thousands line up to give urine samples. On the sound track, the National Anthem rises louder and louder, and we hear the words:

> "Oh, say, does that star spangled banner yet wave
> O'er the LAND OF THE FREE . . . and THE HOME OF THE BRAVE"

CUT TO: CISCO KID *and* PANCHO *riding side by side.*

PANCHO: Is it true you know the Secret of Power, Cisco?

CISCO KID: Indeed. All superheroes and sub-geniuses know the Secret of Power, Pancho.

PANCHO: I know I'm only a sidekick and sidekicks aren't supposed to know the Secret of Power—but—well, we've been together a long time . . .

CISCO KID: Pancho, I shouldn't do this—but you have been a good friend and *chelah* . . . I'll tell you.

PANCHO: Oh, thank you, thank you. What is it?

CISCO KID:	Well, Pancho, you know how dumb the average guy is, right?
PANCHO:	Yes . . .
CISCO KID:	Well, Pancho—mathematically, by definition, half of them are even dumber than that!
PANCHO:	Ha-ha-ha, Cisco!
CISCO KID:	Ha-ha-ha, Pancho!

They gallop off into the sunset.

CUT TO:	*Bumper stickers on cars:*

DON'T TREAD ON ME *(with rattlesnake)*

THE SUM TOTAL OF ALL MINDS IS ONE

I LOVE THE SMELL OF MALATHION IN THE MOONLIGHT

CUT TO:	*Tight closeup of IGNATZ with microphone as TV reporter on a street in Los Angeles.*
IGNATZ:	And so Pancho, knowing the Secret of Power, created his own New Age cult. He is now a millionaire and lives in Malibu.

NARRATOR *walks by holding another microphone, camera slowly follows him.*

IGNATZ:	It began with L. Ron Hubbard. Then J. R. "Bob" Dobbs. Now, Pancho, once a humble sidekick, has become richer than the Pope. (*His voice fades as camera follows NARRATOR.*)
NARRATOR:	The Führer type is not created *only* by his own dominant imprint on the second anal-territorial circuit. For a Führer to exist, there must be masses with a submissive imprint on that circuit.

MIDGET *passes with another microphone going in the other direction. Camera follows him.*

NARRATOR:	Hitler, they say, was a genius at politics. That should tell us what politics is. . . . (*Voice fades as camera moves to follow MIDGET.*)

MIDGET: Some have a robot pro-anchovy imprint, and some have a robot anti-anchovy imprint. Some have a Gay imprint, and some have a straight imprint. But none of them know that they're robots.

SHELLEY *walks by with her own microphone, going in the other direction. Camera follows her.*

MIDGET: Some have a Führer or Guru imprint. Some have a disciple imprint. . . . *(Voice fades.)*

SHELLEY: But we are all really okay because we are all God, you know, and if you have a salary like mine, you can't believe anything is seriously wrong anywhere.

CUT TO: *The TV* ANNOUNCER, *looking uncommonly grim. He holds up an egg.*

ANNOUNCER: One more time. This is your brain.

Drops egg into frying pan, where it sizzles.

ANNOUNCER: This is your brain on drugs. *(Long pause.)* Any questions?

CUT TO: *Audience in TV studio watching* ANNOUNCER.
               NARRATOR *rises out of audience.*

NARRATOR: In what respects is my brain like an egg? Which part is the
               yolk? Which part is the white? What scientific studies demon-
               strate these isomorphisms between my brain and an egg? What
               drugs do you mean? Aspirin, LSD, penicillin, cocaine, caffeine,
               nicotine, Valium, antihistamines, antibiotics? What scientific
               studies show an isomorphism between a frying egg and my
               brain on aspirin? On LSD? On penicillin? What isomorphisms
               specifically were found?

A shot rings out. NARRATOR *falls dead.*

Camera pans back to ANNOUNCER.

ANNOUNCER: There's a wiseass in every crowd. Now (*adding bacon*) this is
               your brain on drugs with two slices of bacon. This is your brain
               on drugs with three slices of bacon.

CUT TO: *More footage from* THIEF OF BAGHDAD. DOUGLAS
               FAIRBANKS *rides a magic carpet above the city.* CROWD
               stares upward in amazement.

FAIRBANKS: A disciple is an asshole looking for a human being to attach itself to!

CROWD: Oh, wise one, may we be *your* disciples?

CUT TO: *A pastel wall with playing card doors on it. ACE OF HEARTS opens and* EISENHOWER *(edited in) appears and waves.*

EISENHOWER: Hi, folks. Haven't things gone to hell since I died?

CUT TO: *Fast forward.*

CUT TO: *The Mercator map of the world again.*

NARRATOR (*voice over*): Once we imprint a semantic circuit—a reality-tunnel made of words and concepts and ideas—human evolution starts to move in quantum waves. Once again, on this projection, we will see six thousand years in one minute—one hundred years a second. Watch.

A yellow blob appears over Cambodia and begins to move west and mildly north rapidly.

NARRATOR: The first quantum leap began around Cambodia and Thailand, where there is a great deal of tin and copper. Somebody discovered that if you throw them in the same furnace, a new synergetic product comes out—bronze. Once the Bronze Age began, humanity quantum-jumped from simple hunting-and-gathering tribes to huge Agricultural Civilizations.

The yellow blob covers Asia and the Mideast and enters Greece and North Africa.

NARRATOR: At the top, there was usually a Sun King—a male, allegedly descended from the Sun God. At the bottom, a horde of slaves captured in battle. The subjugation of women and the invention of slavery mark this kind of civilization for more than four thousand years.

CUT TO: BISHOP *rebuking* LON CHANEY, SR.

BISHOP: No, no, no, Quasimodo—you must *never* think for yourself. You must believe what your Masters tell you.

CHANEY *cringes with guilt.*

CUT TO: *Clips from ALEXANDER NEVSKY—Teutonic Knights on the march.*

Courtesy of the Academy Of Motion Picture Arts & Sciences

NARRATOR (*voice over*): These civilizations made great progress in the arts and sciences, but remained Authoritarian. As late as the 18th Century, Louis XIV was still a Sun King—and the Inquisition handled free thought the way Oriental Despots had three thousand years earlier.

CUT TO: *The Mercator map. The yellow blob now covers most of the world, including parts of North and South America.*

NARRATOR: There were only a few pockets of tribalism left by about 1750, and they were being rapidly absorbed. This process, which has taken about forty seconds on this simulation, required four thousand years of real time.

CUT TO: *Painting of James Watt.*

NARRATOR (*voice over*): In 1765, in Scotland, James Watt was looking at the lid of a pot jumping up and down as the water heated.

CUT TO: *The Mercator map. A red dot appears in Scotland.*

NARRATOR (*voice over*): Watt invented the steam engine, and society took another quantum jump. A new type of civilization began. We were swamped by what Alvin Toffler calls *Industreality.*

The red dot swells into a blob that sweeps over Europe and North America, and then begins to creep into Asia and Africa.

NARRATOR: The first quantum-jump Bronze Age Sun King Civilizations required thousands of years to spread across the world. *Industreality* moved ten times faster and transformed the planet in only two centuries—the two seconds you just saw on this simulation.

    Industreality killed off the Sun Kings and created Democracy. Women's suffrage and labor unions followed in its wake. Radical Utopian Ideas appeared—socialism and anarchism and Partnership Societies based on Native American models, and science-fiction Utopias of all sorts. But war and other problems did not go away, and no Utopia appeared. People lived longer and were healthier than ever before, but Injustices continued, and many weren't sure if the world was getting better or getting worse. The only thing we could be sure of was that it was changing faster than ever.

CUT TO: *Fast forward.*

CUT TO: *Montage of bombed-out cities, Vietnam atrocities, the opening of Nazi Death Camps, atomic tests, computers, graph showing increase in average lifespan, (1750—27 years; 1900—50 years; 1970—72 years; 1990—76 years), Victorian slums contrasted with modern suburbs, then modern slums as bad as the Victorian ones, Ku Klux Klan rally, quick shots of Gay Lib rally, Women's Lib rally, antiwar rally, Berlin Wall being chopped into pieces.*

NARRATOR: Amid unprecedented success, some looked about them and saw only our remaining failures. "Back to the Stone Age" became the unspoken slogan of many radical reactionaries. But meanwhile, *Industreality* itself was being replaced by a third quantum jump.

CUT TO: *Photo of Norbert Wiener, John von Neumann, and Claude Shannon.*

NARRATOR (*voice over*): While *Industreality* was reaching its peak in the years right after World War II, the third quantum wave was being unleashed by Professor Wiener at MIT, Professor von Neumann at Princeton, and Dr. Shannon at Bell Laboratories. We were entering the Information Age.

CUT TO: *The Mercator map. The yellow of Agri/Bronze Civilization has largely been replaced by the red of Industreality. A blue dot appears in the northeast United States, representing the Information Revolution. It spreads very, very quickly (less than one second) across the United States, centers in Northern California, jumps the Pacific to cover Japan, and leaps backward to Europe.*

NARRATOR: The age of the bit and the byte, the age of information acceleration, spread across the world in only decades—ten times faster than Industreality and a hundred times faster than the Sun King Civilizations. The trajectory remains Fast Westward, Fast Forward.

CUT TO: *The Earth floating in space. Red dots begin to appear making orbits—and their numbers increase very rapidly.*

NARRATOR (*voice over*): Now, having circumnavigated the globe like the Norway rat, much of our communication technology is in Outer Space, and more is moving there every week. The trajectory is becoming Fast Forward and Fast Outward—to the stars.

Subtitle: **UTOPIA OR OBLIVION**

CUT TO: *Montage of computers, Nelson Mandela leaving prison, comput-*
               ers, Vaclav Havel addressing Congress, computers, Space Shuttle
               launching.

CUT TO: *Montage of recent books on longevity: LIFE EXTENSION by*
               Pearson and Shaw, HERE COMES IMMORTALITY by
               Tucille, PROLONGEVITY by Rosenfeld, THE CONQUEST
               OF DEATH by Silverman, NO MORE DYING by Kurtzman
               and Gordon, THE IMMORTALIST by Harrington.

NARRATOR: As Buckminster Fuller said, we are now standing between Uto-
               pia and Oblivion.

CUT TO: *Bumper stickers on cars:*

KILL A COMMIE FOR CHRIST

WHERE IS LEE HARVEY OSWALD NOW THAT WE NEED HIM?

I BRAKE FOR ANIMALS

DEATH TO ALL FANATICS!

I BRAKE FOR HALLUCINATIONS

ARM THE HOMELESS—
RIOT AT CITY HALL NEW YEAR'S EVE

I BRAKE FOR SHOGGOTHS

I SMOKE MARIJUANA
AND I VOTE, MR. BUSH

CUT TO: *Footage from THE OUTLAW. BILLY THE KID and JANE RUSSELL are wrestling on the floor of a stable.*

JANE: Please don't—please . . .

BILLY (*in Bogart's voice*):   When a man's partner is shot, he's supposed to do something about it.

JANE: But I thought Victor died in a concentration camp.

BILLY: Well, yeah, but then there were the strawberries.

JANE: You're just looking for an excuse to rape somebody.

BILLY: Well, there ain't nobody else here but the *horses*.

JANE *breaks loose and threatens him with a pitchfork.*

JANE: Sisterhood is powerful!

NARRATOR (*voice over*): Well, that was Hollywood sex in the forties. Billy did rape Jane, but she liked it. Can you *believe* that? Sam Spade never did find that damned black bird. Meanwhile, the fourth quantum jump is already beginning—nanotechnology, which will change the world faster and more totally than the agricultural, industrial, and information revolutions.

CUT TO: SCIENTIST *in white lab smock earnestly addressing camera. Caption identifies him as* SCIENTIFIC AUTHORITY.

SCIENTIST: Millions of molecule-size computers will be produced in this generation. Once a replicator molecule is created, it can make 28 trillion copies of itself—similar nanocomputers—in about ten hours.

NARRATOR (*voice over*): What about nanomedicine, doctor?

SCIENTIST: Well, it seems to some of us that disease is about to be abolished and longevity is knocking on our door. Molecular computers can enter every cell in the body, hunting diseased cells and repairing them from the inside. Persons in cryonic suspension can be revived as soon as this technology is on line. That means potential immortality.

NARRATOR (*voice over*): How soon do you think nanotechnology will be, as you say, on line?

SCIENTIST: Different researchers estimate the time differently. I'd guess ten to fifteen years.

NARRATOR: And what country has the heaviest investment in this research?

SCIENTIST: At present, Japan.

CUT TO: *Mercator map. Re-run in fast speed of all previous East-West trajectories, each projected forward a bit to climax in Japan.*

CUT TO: *Footage from Frank Capra's MEET JOHN DOE.* GARY
               COOPER *addressing a mass rally at Madison Square Garden.*

COOPER: No loyal American would resent giving a urine sample to the
               government. I want you good folks to go right home after this
               meeting, and take a hearty piss, and mail it to George Bush at
               the White House.

Long shot of CROWD, *angry, throwing tomatoes at* COOPER.

CUT TO: *Closeup of the sign in the public park:*

NO PUBLIC IN

THE PUBLIC PARK

CUT TO: *Conference room.* ANNOUNCER *sits behind desk, playing* *Boss. Caption identifies him as* TOP DOG.

IGNATZ *stands nervously, waiting. Caption identifies him as* BOTTOM DOG.

ANNOUNCER: Well, first the good news, Dagwood, and then the bad news. (*He looks at papers while* IGNATZ *cringes.*) Your urine test was absolutely drug free.

IGNATZ: Well, of course, Mr. Dithers, I wouldn't . . .

ANNOUNCER: Unfortunately, I am sorry to say our doctors found traces of hoof and mouth disease. You will have to be put down before you infect the rest of the herd.

CUT TO: *Nazi storm troopers dragging* IGNATZ *down the long dark hall to a door marked* DEATH OF EGO.

CUT TO: *Bumper stickers on cars:*

THEY'LL TAKE AWAY MY GUN WHEN
THEY PRY MY COLD DEAD FINGERS FROM THE TRIGGER

HONK IF YOU LOVE CTHULHU

INTELLIGENCE IS THE ULTIMATE APHRODISIAC

THERE IS NO SUCH THING AS
A NONWORKING MOTHER

THE UNIVERSE IS LAUGHING
BEHIND YOUR BACK

CUT TO: *Footage of* CISCO KID *and* PANCHO *riding across the desert.*
                 This time CISCO KID *has a French accent and sounds like*
                 Charles Boyer. PANCHO *has the rolling Dublin brogue of Barry*
                 Fitzgerald.

PANCHO: Why can't we have cars like everybody else? This gallop-gal-
                 lop-gallop everywhere is a stiff pain the arse. And I mean that
                 literally.

CISCO KID: Cars create air pollution, Pancho. Have you ever looked closely
                 at what comes out of the back of a car?

PANCHO: Oh, begorrah, Cisco, if you've become a bleedin' environmen-
                 talist suddenly, did you ever look closely at all, at all, at what
                 comes out the back of our horses?

CISCO KID: Pancho, sometimes I think you should have your head candled.

CUT TO: *Conference room. NARRATOR (in tropical suit) and ANNOUNCER (in white lab smock) look at blackboard with Schrödinger's wave equation on it. On the table is a can of soup labeled* FRENCH COLUMBIAN BROADCASTING SYSTEM.

ANNOUNCER: So the wave function never collapses, and every eigenstate is equally real, in this theory?

NARRATOR: Exactly. There might be universes in which Hitler never went into politics and is remembered only as a banal landscape painter.

ANNOUNCER: And a universe in which John Baez is not a general but something else—a poet, a grocer, maybe even a pacifist activist?

NARRATOR: And a universe in which General Baez isn't male at all, but female. He might be called Joan Baez over there.

ANNOUNCER: And a universe in which George Washington was never assassinated?

NARRATOR: Certainly. And a universe where Kennedy didn't elope to Mexico with Marilyn Monroe but stayed on as President and got assassinated instead of Nixon.

ANNOUNCER *(after a long thoughtful pause)*: Sure makes you think, this modern physics.

CUT TO: *The garden scene. ZEN MASTER sits in Lotus Position; MONK enters and bows.*

ZEN MASTER: Have you discovered the Great One who makes the grass green?

MONK *(desperately)*: The grass is green of itself. That is its self-ness—its greenness is self-ness.

ZEN MASTER *bops him again with the staff. Large BAM KA-ZAM onscreen.*

CUT TO: *Conference room with* ANNOUNCER, NARRATOR, *and* FATTEST ACTRESS. *On the table is a can of soup labeled* FIVE CONSECRATED BAVARIAN SEERS.

ANNOUNCER: I don't know—I'm just not sure it'll work.

NARRATOR: I'm sure it'll be okay if we leave off the anchovies.

IGNATZ *and* BETTY, *in pajamas and negligee, burst through door.*

IGNATZ: What the fuck you guys doing to our TV? You a buncha commies or libertarians or something?

BETTY (*looking at* NARRATOR):   That one looks like an extraterrestrial.

Wall collapses inward, and MIDGET *breaks in through the rubble.*

MIDGET: Gonad shall have a bride!

He grabs BETTY *and they struggle.*

CUT TO: *Closeup of the Bible, open to Romans, chapter 8, verses 14 to 17. On soundtrack, faintly, the opening bars of Beethoven's "Ode to Joy."*

BETTY (*solemnly*): For as many as are led by the Spirit of God, they are the sons of God.
        Ye have not received the spirit of bondage again to fear; but ye have received the spirit of adoption, whereby we cry, Abba, Father.
        The Spirit beareth witness with our spirit, that we are the children of God, and if children, then heirs, heirs of God and

joint-heirs with Christ.

CUT TO: *Closeup of Austrian 1000-Schilling note with picture of*
                  SCHRÖDINGER.. SCHRÖDINGER *opens his mouth and*
                  speaks.

SCHRÖDINGER: Mind simply does not exist in the plural. The sum total of all
                  minds is One.

Sound: *Beethoven's "Ode to Joy," a slight bit louder.*

CUT TO: *The two arrows from Gestalt psychology that are the same length*

but look different due to the arrangement of points at their ends.

NARRATOR: Here's a hint about the Great One who makes the grass green.
                  These two arrows are actually the same length. As Nietzsche
                  said, we are all greater artists than we realize.

CUT TO: *ILLUMINATI poster.*

Bavarian Illuminati

Founded by Hassan i Sabbah, 1090 A.D. (5090 A.L., 4850 A.M.)
Reformed by Adam Weishaupt, 1776 A.D. (5776 A.L., 5536 A.M.)

THE ANCIENT ILLUMINATED SEERS OF BAVARIA

invite YOU to join

The World's Oldest and Most Successful Conspiracy

Don't Let THEM Immanentize the Eschaton

Have you ever SECRETLY WONDERED WHY the GREAT PYRAMID has FIVE sides (counting the bottom)?

WHAT IS the TRUE secret SINISTER REALITY lying behind the ANCIENT Aztec Legend of QUETZALCOATL?

WHO IS the MAN in ZURICH that some SWEAR is **LEE HARVEY OSWALD**?

IS there an ESOTERIC ALLEGORY concealed in the apparently innocent legend of Snow White and the Seven Dwarfs?

WHY do scholarly anthropologists TURN PALE with terror at the very MENTION of the FORBIDDEN name YOG-SOTHOTH?

WHAT REALLY DID HAPPEN TO AMBROSE BIERCE?

If your I.Q. is over 150, and you have $3,125.00 (plus handling), you **might** be eligible for a trial membership in the A.I.S.B. If you think you qualify, put the money in a cigar box and bury it in your backyard. One of our Underground Agents will contact you shortly.

I DARE YOU!

TELL NO ONE: ACCIDENTS HAVE A STRANGE WAY OF HAPPENING TO PEOPLE WHO TALK TOO MUCH ABOUT THE BAVARIAN ILLUMINATI!

May we warn you against imitations!
Ours is the original and genuine

"NOTHING IS TRUE. EVERYTHING IS PERMISSIBLE." –Hassan i Sabbah

Nil Carborundum Illegitimo

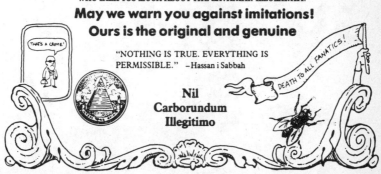

CUT TO: *Closeup of the Bible, open to John, chapter 10, verse 34.*

BETTY *(reading solemnly)*: Jesus answered them, "Is it not written, I said, ye are Gods?"

Sound: *Beethoven's "Ode to Joy" coming in stronger, louder.*

CUT TO: NARRATOR *sitting behind table with Inner Quest brain machine before him.*

NARRATOR: With these buttons you can program any trip you want. The wave forms you create go directly to the brain, and you enter that level of meditation or trance. Up here, you put in any tape you want—your favorite music—and you trance out on the music just as if you were listening to it on pot. And this isn't illegal. Or, you put in a hypno-tape, say a Stop Worrying tape, or a Success tape, and as you go into trance, the tape programs your subconscious. *You can be anybody you want to be, the next time around.*

CUT TO: *Fast forward.*

CUT TO: *The Mercator map again.*

NARRATOR *(voice over)*:   The acceleration of knowledge was calculated a few
                years ago by French statistician Georges Anderla. On this com-
                puter simulation, one minute again equals six thousand years.
                The Bronze Age began in Asia and moved Fast Westward, Fast
                Forward. By A.D. 1 the center of power and knowledge was the
                city of Rome, seat of the Roman Empire—the largest Sun King-
                dom known until that time. Call all the information known at
                that time one anderla.

A dot appears over Rome.

NARRATOR: It took fifteen hundred years for information to double. By
                then, the seat of knowledge and power was in the universities
                and banks of Northern Italy—and the Renaissance was in full
                swing. Leonardo was about forty years old.

A dot, twice as big as the first, appears over Northern Italy.

NARRATOR: The next doubling took only 250 years and occurred mostly in
                England, "the first Empire on which the sun never set."

A third dot twice as big as the second appears over England.

NARRATOR: The Inquisition had stopped thought in Southern Europe, but
                any educated person in England could, in 1750, know twice as
                much as anybody in Florence in 1500 or four times as much as
                anybody in Rome in A.D. 1. The next doubling took 150 years,
                while the center of knowledge and power moved to Wall Street
                and the Ivy League colleges of our Northeast. By 1900, America
                was replacing England as world leader.

A dot twice the size of the last one, or eight times the first one, appears over New York/New England.

NARRATOR: And the next doubling took only fifty years and was complete by 1950.

The biggest dot yet appears over Chicago.

NARRATOR: But then the acceleration accelerated even more.

In 0.1 second a dot twice as big as last appears over UC Berkeley; 0.07 seconds later a dot twice as big as that over CalTech; in 0.06 seconds more a dot twice as big as that appears over the Pacific Ocean, covering parts of California and Japan.

NARRATOR: Knowledge doubled again by 1960, again by 1967, and again by 1973. Now it is doubling every eighteen months and moving into space satellites—which will soon be Space Cities.

CUT TO: ANNOUNCER *and* NARRATOR *in conference room.*

ANNOUNCER: What percentage of American astronauts showed alterations in consciousness?

NARRATOR: Eighty to 85 percent.

ANNOUNCER: And Russian cosmonauts?

NARRATOR: The same—80 to 85 percent. Entering zero gravity is a re-imprinting experience.

CUT TO: *The* MIDGET *sitting beneath a tree.*

MIDGET (*thoughtfully*): In 1928, one man flew the Atlantic. In 1978—fifty years later—two hundred million people flew the Atlantic. Projecting that forward into space, how many millions will be leaving the planet in 2028?

NARRATOR *(voice over)*: A few hundred million at least—and 80 to 85 percent will undergo "rebirth" or re-imprinting or a new reality-tunnel or a new ego or some kind of so-called "mystic" alteration in consciousness.

Soundtrack: *"Ode to Joy," softly but insistently.*

CUT TO: *Animation of brain releasing peptides.*

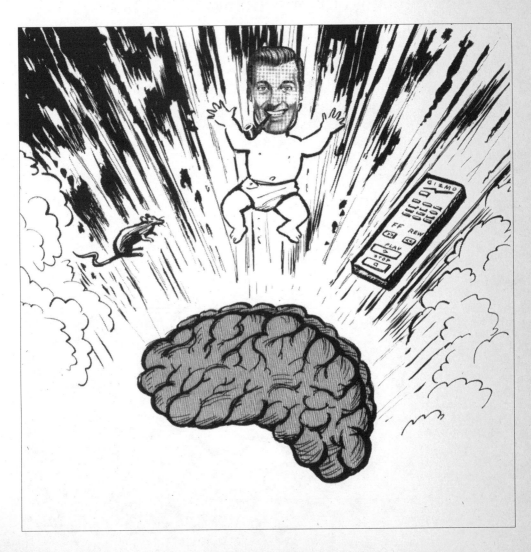

NARRATOR *(voice over)*: A re-imprinting experience, whether with psychedelics or brain machines or isolation tanks or going into zero gravity, means new networks in the brain.

CUT TO: *Bumper stickers on cars:*

YOG SOTHOTH NEBLOD ZIN

EVERY DECENT MAN IS ASHAMED OF HIS GOVERNMENT

GENERIC BUMPER STICKER

WHOEVER DIES WITH THE MOST TOYS WINS

CUT TO: KUNG FU CLASS *in training.*

NARRATOR *(voice over)*: If you want to change your first-circuit reality-tunnel— the biosurvival imprints—take up some martial art like karate or kung fu.

CUT TO: *An* ENCOUNTER GROUP.

NARRATOR *(voice over)*: If you want to change your second-circuit reality-tunnel—the ego defenses and territorial imprints—try an Encounter Group.

CUT TO: A PHILOSOPHY ADDICT *being sentenced by the court.*

NARRATOR *(voice over)*: If you want to change your third-circuit reality-tunnel—your verbal and conceptual imprints—try studying comparative religion and philosophy.

CUT TO: COPS *questioning* PHILOSOPHY ADDICT.

COP #1:   And this is another sad case of the effects of Advanced Philosophy courses. This woman started out with Pure Logic and got involved in the paradox of the barber who shaves every man who doesn't shave himself. Then she moved on to the Hard Stuff—Bertrand Russell's class of all classes that do not include themselves, which includes itself if it doesn't, but doesn't include itself if it does. Then she moved on to mind-altering books—quantum mechanics and the cat who is dead and alive at the same time.

Closeup of the gibbering PHILOSOPHY ADDICT, *a hopeless idiot.*

COP #2:   We must be merciful in a case like this. I would sentence her to five years of watching Donahue and Geraldo reruns. That should bring her back to consensus reality.

CUT TO:　　　　*Footage from THE THIRD MAN. JOSEPH COTTEN, drunk, staggers about a Vienna street, the weaving camera helping to create the drunken perspective, and shouts at a HIDDEN FIGURE in a doorway.*

COTTEN:　　　　So the cat *is* dead and alive at the same time—and the Zen Master does and does not change the light bulb—in different universes. And our thoughts, our chemical brain networks, determine which universe we go into—is that what you're trying to tell us? Or is this all bullshit? Come out, come out, and let us see your face, and 'fess up now, 'fess up.

Light comes on in window and illuminates the smiling, enigmatic, inscrutable face of ORSON WELLES.

CUT TO: *Closeup of the Bible, open to I John, chapter 3, verse 2.*

BETTY *(voice over, solemnly)*:   Beloved, now we are the sons of God, and it doth not appear what we shall be.
     But we know that when He shall appear, we shall be like Him, for we shall see Him as he is.

Sound: *"Ode to Joy" grows louder.*

CUT TO: NARRATOR *walking in the woodland scene.*

NARRATOR: If you don't like the fourth-circuit reality-tunnel—your sexual imprints—come to Los Angeles. If you want to change all your imprints at once, sign up now to join the first Space Colony and enter a totally new reality-tunnel.

CUT TO: *Camera zooming through solar system, then rising suddenly to confront billions of stars. We pan upward and see beyond our galaxy to billions of other galaxies. "Ode to Joy" builds toward its climax.*

CUT TO: ANNOUNCER *addressing audience.*

ANNOUNCER: But if you want to adjust to society—act like a dumbshit, and
                   everybody will treat you as an equal.

Caption: PARTNERSHIP FOR A BRAIN-FREE AMERICA

CUT TO: BETTY *standing by yellow wall with Sacred Chao symbol on it.*

BETTY: O nobly born, you who are about to experience re-imprinting
                   in Discordian wisdom and higher brain circuits, look upon the
                   Sacred Chao. *(This is pronounced kayow.)*

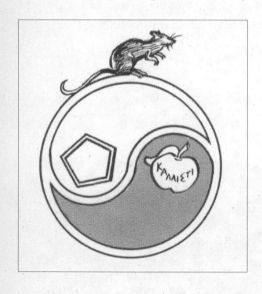

Caption: CHAO: ONE UNIT OF CHAOS

BETTY: This is the symbol of the polarity of all human experience, male and female, yang and yin, sweet and sour, Republicrat and Democan. Basically, though it is the eternal Hodge and the eternal Podge in dynamic balance. Here, on the Hodge side *(pointing)* is the Golden Apple of Eris, the Forbidden Fruit of Eve, the symbol of all dark, earthy, anarchistic forces. It is also the apple which used to disappear from the stage of the Flatbush Burlesque House in Brooklyn when Peaches La Rue did the split on top of it at the climax of her striptease. And here on the Podge side *(pointing)* is the Pentagon, symbol of werewolves, the Military Industrial Complex, and all the bright, efficient bureaucracies on the planet.

    The Secret of Power, O nobly born, is that every increase in Podge or efficiency or militarism or higher taxes leads to an increase in Hodge or rebellion or anarchy or tax evasion; and every increase in civil or uncivil disobedience leads to an increase in cops and courts and jails and more efficiency. Imposition of order always equals escalation of chaos and escalation of chaos equals imposition of order. The Sacred Chao remains in perpetual wobble, never in stasis.

BETTY *holds up an apple.*

BETTY: And Our Lady Eris has left us a symbol of this Truth in the very structure of the apple itself, the symbol of Disobedience. Cut any apple open, and what do you see?

She cuts open the apple, and we see the seeds in their eternal pentagon shape.

BETTY: Inside every Hodge is a bit of Authoritarian Podge, and inside every bureaucratic Podge is pure chaotic Hodge. And this is another proof of the Law of Fives, by the way.

CUT TO: *Closeup of* ANNOUNCER *with head of J. R. "Bob" Dobbs on wall behind him.*

ANNOUNCER: BULLSHIT, bullshit, *bullshit*. The world does *not* consist of Hodge and Podge—or yin and yang—or positive and negative—or any of those other abstractions invented by mystics and scientists. Concretely, if you look around, you'll see the world consists of a little Something and a vast amount of Nothing. Look at me. I'm Something. All around me is a lot of Nothing. Look at my hand *(waving it)*—that's Something, too, but all around it is vast abysses of Nothing. Anything you examine is Something, but it's always surrounded by a hell of a lot more of Nothing. Am I right? You bet your ass. As "Bob" tells us in *The Book of the Sub-Genius*—Praise "Bob"!—

VOICES *(offscreen)*: Praise "Bob"! Praise "Bob"!

ANNOUNCER: —the whole Secret of Power lies in the balance of Something and Nothing. If you want Eternal Salvation *or triple your money back*, let Slack into your aorta, and let "Bob" into your bank account, and you, too, can have the peace of knowing Truth. Slack is the midpoint between Something and Nothing. Then, in true Slack, you can get Something for Nothing!

VOICES: Praise "Bob"! Praise "Bob"!

VOICE #1:   Praise "Bob"!

VOICE #2:   Is this the Church of Scientology?

VOICE #3:   Who's got the Frop?

CUT TO: *Footage from Merian C. Cooper's THE MOST DANGEROUS GAME. JOEL and FAY are running through jungle hunted by the MAD BARON.*

FAY: What the hell happened to Bruce Cabot? And who the hell are you, mister?

JOEL: Bruce got a hernia. Mr. Cooper asked me to take over for him.

FAY: Christ Jesus, do you think you can handle that big monkey?

JOEL: Certainly. I've got Slack. Praise "Bob"!

FAY: What are you, some kinda religious nut?

NARRATOR (*voice over*): Politics and show business began to merge when George
                Murphy, a musical comedy star, got elected to the U.S. Senate.
                Next, Eisenhower hired Robert Montgomery—an actor, direc-
                tor and producer of vast talent and Republican sympathies—to
                coach him on how to act for television. Eisenhower was our
                first Media President. Then Ronald Reagan used the same tech-
                niques, and polls repeatedly showed that, while the majority of
                Americans disliked most of Reagan's policies, they "liked" and
                "approved" him. Image had replaced reality. Now Clint
                Eastwood and Sonny Bono are in politics. How long will it take
                before the Democrats gets wise and we have all-Hollywood
                government with Paul Newman as President, Barbra Streisand
                as VP, and Lassie as Secretary of Agriculture?

Caption: SATIRE. *This is crossed out and replaced by the word* PROPHECY.

CUT TO: ANNOUNCER *at TV news desk.*

ANNOUNCER: Yes, new neurological circuits are forming all over the planet.
                Reports say people everywhere are learning to use their brains for
                fun and profit. We have learned more about brain change in the
                last decade than in all previous history. Scientists debate whether
                this is a just another historical quantum jump or a genuine
                evolutionary transformation, but those in the forefront of the
                mutation say it was foreseen by Nietzsche a hundred years ago.

CUT TO: NIETZSCHE *hiking in the high Alps.*

NIETZSCHE: What is humanity? A bridge between the ape and the Super-
                Human—a bridge over an abyss.

CUT TO: ZEN MASTER *in the garden.* MONK *approaches, bows.*

ZEN MASTER: Well? Have you found the Great One who makes the grass green?

MONK (*with blissful certitude*): I am!

ZEN MASTER: And who is that "I"?

MONK: There is only one "I."

CUT TO: *Austrian 1000-Schilling note in animation.* SCHRÖDINGER's *picture speaks again.*

SCHRÖDINGER: The sum total of all minds is One.

BETTY (*voice over*): And God said unto Moses I AM WHO I AM. Say unto the children of Israel, I AM hath sent me.

CUT TO: IGNATZ *in hall, opens door marked* THE WAY OUT.

CUT TO: *Flames cover the screen.*

BETTY (*voice over*): For the earnest expectation of the creature awaiteth the manifestation of the sons of God.

CUT TO: *Two-minute montage of nature scenery as "Ode to Joy" moves toward its climax. We see waterfalls, deserts, trees, beavers, birds, tropical flowers, lakes, mountains, starry sky, intricately designed insects, dogs playing, faces of infants of all races, sunset behind the Taj Mahal.*

CUT TO: NARRATOR *in front of blank white screen.*

NARRATOR: We make the grass green. We make the world beautiful—or we make it ugly. We make it cheerful or depressing. The end of the Valley of Decision is the one word, *choice.* Bucky Fuller said we stand between Utopia and Oblivion. We stand also between pro-choice and anti-choice—personally, nationally, internationally. Design your own reality-tunnel today. Remember, reality is what you can get away with, and if you can't get away with it, it just ain't real.

CUT TO: *Sound: The "Ode to Joy" moves to its thundering climax as we
                 see a montage.*

CUT TO: BUSH *and* QUAYLE *at a political rally.*

BUSH: Say good night, Dan.

QUAYLE: "Good night, Dan."

Titles roll.

NARRATOR: And God bless us every one.